Inside you'll meet such unforgettable felines as . . .

Priscilla, who inexplicably meowed at her apartment door for two days, until her perplexed owners thought to check on their elderly neighbor and discovered that she had broken her hip and was unable to move.

Pearl and Skittles, the Keystone Cats, who watched over their household with such total vigilance that any problem—from a clogged drain to a stereo left playing at night—would cause them to wake everyone in the house.

Murry, the cat whose devotion to a young boy with cystic fibrosis was so complete that his own reason for living seemed to depend on the survival of his youthful charge.

Nicholas, who every day fed the family pit bull a dog bone and was rewarded when later his pal would happily lick the cat's head for ten minutes.

Elvira, the "unreliable" black cat, who kept an abandoned baby alive through a freezing, snowy night, confirming a young girl's conviction—and converting her father's skepticism—that the cat had a very good reason for not coming home on schedule.

Subway, the orange tabby who not only survived being shot with a shotgun, but later, apparently killed in an accident, jumped out of the box he was to be buried in and frolicked among the guests at his own funeral.

Also by Michael Capuzzo and Teresa Banik Capuzzo

Our Best Friends:
Wagging Tales to Warm the Heart

Cat Caught My Heart

Purrfect Tales of Wisdom, Hope, and Love

Michael Capuzzo
&
Teresa Banik Capuzzo

BANTAM BOOKS

NEW YORK   TORONTO   LONDON   SYDNEY   AUCKLAND

This edition contains the complete text of
the original hardcover edition.
NOT ONE WORD HAS BEEN OMITTED.

CAT CAUGHT MY HEART
A Bantam Book

PUBLISHING HISTORY
Bantam hardcover edition published March 1998
Bantam paperback edition / July 1999

Please see pages 271–274 for permissions.

ISBN 0-553-58101-5

Published simultaneously in the United States and Canada

Bantam Books are published by Bantam Books, a division of
Random House, Inc. Its trademark, consisting of the words
"Bantam Books" and the portrayal of a rooster, is
Registered in U.S. Patent and Trademark Office and in
other countries. Marca Registrada. Bantam Books, 1540
Broadway, New York, New York 10036.

PRINTED IN THE UNITED STATES OF AMERICA

OPM   10 9 8 7 6 5 4 3 2 1

This book is dedicated to former strays Texas, Argo, Lander, and Daisy, and the wonderful places they came to us from: America's animal shelters.

Contents

Introduction

No one should waste time trying to define mankind's relationship to the cat. That task defies us even as the cats themselves do. Maybe the cats themselves understand it, maybe they don't either, but it doesn't matter all that much. What does matter is that on a planet where most of the life forms that evolved over billions of years are now extinct, some higher wisdom decided to let us and our cats coexist at the same moment in history. What has resulted from that cherished coincidence is a unique kind of love.

Love and mystery are practically synonymous in our culture and cats are just about the most mysterious critters we interact with. (Snakes may be as mysterious but very few people love snakes. They are interested in them. Cats have a much higher cuddle factor than snakes.) Anyway, when it comes to cats and our deep appreciation of them, love and mystery become all wrapped up in each other, and we are in the grasp of both. And don't we just love it!

Mike and Teresa Capuzzo, devoted life-and-living-things lovers, have explored the cat/human equation by seeking out and recording events that have happened to real people interacting with real cats. What results may seem otherworldly, but these stories (dare I say tales?) are very real as you are about to learn.

—Roger A. Caras
Thistle Hill Farm

CHAPTER ONE

On Love

People may surprise you with unexpected kindness. Dogs have a depth of loyalty that often we seem unworthy of. But the love of a cat is a blessing and a privilege in this world.

—**Kinky Friedman**

I think back on the strange views that many people held about cats. They were selfish creatures reserving their affections only for situations which would benefit them, and they were incapable of the unthinking love a dog dispenses. They were totally self-contained creatures who looked after their own interests only. What nonsense! I have felt cats rubbing their faces against mine and touching my cheek with claws carefully sheathed. These things, to me, are expressions of love.

—**James Herriot**

Barney: A True Story of an Old Lady and Her Cat

Barney was a most unusual cat. He wasn't of any particular breed, just a stray that someone had tossed from a car in the woods at the bottom of my lane. He was about three months old when I found him—just a little thing crying in the woods. He was thin, scared, and hungry. I picked him up, carried him home; and in a few weeks he became, to me, the most beautiful cat I had ever seen.

Barney came to me at a crucial time in my life. My husband had died very suddenly of a heart attack three months before, and I was alone. It often amazed me that right about the time my husband died, Barney was born. Everyone needs someone to love and care for, and Barney became the most important part of my life.

Perhaps I loved Barney too much, but I had someone to get up for again in the morning, someone to feed and care for, but most important someone to love and someone to love me.

Barney was a red-and-orange tiger, often called a marmalade. His markings were perfect, and the stripes on each of his sides formed a bull's-eye. The children in the neighborhood often remarked what an excellent target he would make, but in the rural section of Bucks County, Pennsylvania, where I live, the children love and respect animals, so I didn't have to worry about Barney being hurt.

Barney had the most mischievous face and the brightest eyes I had ever seen on any cat, and he lived up to his face! It was very embarrassing when I had guests, to open the dish closet and find him sitting on the plates, and even more upsetting after dinner when I opened the dishwasher and pulled out the rack to have him jump in the back where I couldn't reach him. There he would sit until he was good and ready to come out.

Barney never ate like an ordinary cat. He used his paw for a spoon. He would scoop up his food and eat from his paw. He never slept like other cats with his face buried in his fur. He slept like a person, stretched out full length with his head on my pillow at the top of my bed.

Barney was not allowed out at night. He slept in my bed and every morning just as it began to get light he would awaken me and I would let him out. I think he must have had built-in radar. At ten o'clock, almost to the minute, he would come home for breakfast. Then he would go out again, checking in and out all day just to make sure I was home. The days I went out I would find him sitting in front of the garage anxiously awaiting my return. I would scoop him up in my arms, put him over my shoulder, and with that sleepy look of love on his face, he would purr so excitedly my neck would become all wet.

Barney loved to hunt—not mice, rabbits, or birds like any ordinary cat. Snakes were Barney's favorite. He brought home twelve that first summer—big ones, little ones, thin ones, thick ones, all kinds and all colors— and laid each one at my kitchen door. And Barney loved feathers. He would spend hours playing with them. I often thought Barney pulled the feathers from the tails of our wild guinea hens and pheasants as he stalked them through the fields. Barney's life was one adventure after another.

Barney was a born clown. Word went around the church that at my home there was always a floor show following dinner. Barney would climb on the back of the sofa and chairs and if any old lady had on a hair net, or earrings, Barney would manage to pull them off. One old lady swears to this day that Barney blew in her ear every time she visited. No one ever got angry. He was picked up, hugged, stroked, and kissed; and he loved every minute of it. Once when he jumped on the tea table and upset all the refreshments, the only remark made was, "Well, that's our Barney."

Every evening as I watched television, Barney would climb in my lap, put his little head on my shoulder, purr, and sleep. At those times he was no longer a cat. He was my baby, my little boy, and my heart filled with love.

One Saturday, late in September, he went out as usual. At ten o'clock he did not come home for breakfast. At noon, I had a premonition something had happened to him and I started looking for him. I called all of my neighbors and asked them to check their cars, garages, and barns, in case he had wandered in and the doors closed. Saturday night passed. It began to rain. I left the garage open and the lights on. I missed church on Sunday and enlisted the help of my neighbors. Everyone was looking for Barney. We walked the highway, through the fields and woods. Monday passed.

On Tuesday evening, just about dusk, my neighbor's young son came to the kitchen door. He looked as though he had been crying. "I found Barney," he said. I looked at him. "He's dead, isn't he?" He nodded. I followed him down the road to the edge of the woods, and there partially hidden by a mound of wet autumn leaves was the broken body of my beloved Barney. I never knew how or why he died. I picked him up, carried him home, and buried him in the garden.

That night I knelt by my bed and with tears streaming down my face asked that age-old question: "Why, God, why? Why Barney? Why Barney, who brought so much laughter and happiness to so many people—old people who had almost forgotten how to laugh?" And as I knelt there crying a feeling of peace came over me and it was then I knew. I knew where Barney was. I knew that Barney would live forever in my heart and in the hearts of all who knew him. And somehow I feel that as I approach the golden gate on my last journey, Barney will be sitting there waiting with that anxious look on his precious little face.

I thanked God for the little time I had him, wiped the tears from my face, and wrote my "Memorial to Barney."

MEMORIAL TO BARNEY
Lord Jesus was checking Heaven one day
Walking along on the bright Milky Way.
He said to himself, "Heaven seems very dull,
The angels are grumbling, all is not well."
He paused for a moment and then looked down
And saw little Barney, my precious clown
With his mischievous face and bright little eyes
And he lifted him gently up to the skies.
He gave him a crown of diamonds and gold
And welcomed him in the heavenly fold.

Now Heaven is not the same as before
For as soon as Barney got through the door
He pushed off his crown on the golden stairs
And climbed on the angels and purred in their ears.
He pulled the feathers from out of their wings
(Feathers were Barney's favorite playthings)
And he almost toppled down from afar.
As he tried to grab a twinkling star.
He keeps pushing his crown around the floor
And his tail gets caught in the golden door.

The angels are busy as they can be
Trying to keep up with little Barney.

He has brightened up Heaven, that I know
But oh, little Barney, I miss you so!

—Evelyn B. Kruse, Age 88

A Lesson in Love

Mr. Vinsley was one of the most memorable clients I've ever known. Originally from England, he was an older man who had been a widower for many years and lived in a beautiful mansion in Kentucky.

"My problem is very unusual," he said at the beginning of our phone call, but he refused to go into any greater detail.

"Please, Mr. Vinsley," I urged him, "I prefer to have an idea of what behavior a cat is displaying in case I feel a visit to the vet is needed."

"I promise you, a vet is not required for this situation," he replied. Pausing a moment, he added, "I assure you, I'm not a crackpot."

I began to discuss my fee with him, but he interrupted again. "It doesn't matter—I'll pay whatever you charge."

I explained to him that if I got to his house and I felt

a vet visit was required, I'd have to reschedule our session. He agreed.

Four days later I was headed to Kentucky.

The Vinsley residence was located on a beautiful and secluded road. The long driveway led up to a magnificent house. There were two cars parked in the driveway—a shining black Mercedes and a dusty gray Honda. I parked next to the Honda.

I was greeted at the door by the housekeeper. She eyed my armful of cat toys and raised an eyebrow.

"I'm the feline behavior consultant," I said with a smile.

"The cat *shrink*," she corrected me.

I was led into the living room, where I was told Mr. Vinsley would join me shortly. I sat down on the huge couch and glanced around the antique-filled room. Massive pieces of furniture dominated the long walls. Each vase and statue looked as if it held a fascinating history. Heavy draperies hung from the large windows, blocking the sun. I felt as if I were in a museum.

While I waited for Mr. Vinsley to appear, I neatly arranged all my cat toys on the carpet next to the couch. My notebook was opened, and my pen sat ready to take down client history. All I needed was my client. So I waited. And waited. My client was now twelve minutes late.

The housekeeper reappeared in the doorway. "Mr. Vinsley apologizes for the delay. He'll be with you directly," she said coolly. "Would you care for something to drink?"

"No, thank you," I replied, and the housekeeper disappeared quickly.

Another ten minutes went by. I found myself starting to get sleepy. The sofa was quite comfortable and the room rather dark. "I'll give him five more minutes and then I'm leaving," I said to myself, or at least I *thought* I'd said it to myself.

"Forgive me, Miss Johnson."

I jerked my head up and looked in the direction of the voice with the British accent. In the doorway stood a very distinguished, thin man in a three-piece suit. I guessed his age to be late seventies. He had a full head of silver hair, combed very stylishly. He stepped toward me, offering his hand. "Please forgive my rudeness," he said as we greeted each other. "I had to take a very important but rather annoying phone call."

"I understand." I nodded. "Now, why don't we get started?"

I began to reach for my notebook, but he stood up and started for the door.

"Let's have some tea," he said. "Or would you prefer coffee?"

I started to say that I had already declined his housekeeper's offer, but he wouldn't take no for an answer. So tea it was.

As we drank our tea and ate cookies baked by the housekeeper (who shot me another skeptical look when she brought in the tray), I began to question Mr. Vinsley about his cat. "What behavior has your cat been displaying?" I asked, preparing to take notes.

"Oh, he's a fine cat," he stated as he took a bite of cookie. "There's nothing wrong with his behavior."

I looked up from my notebook. "There's *nothing* wrong with his behavior?"

He saw my reaction and leaned back in his chair. "I do have a problem with my cat, but it doesn't have anything to do with his behavior."

"All right, then. How can I help you?" I was tempted to remind him that I was, after all, a feline *behavior* consultant, but there was something about this man I liked. He seemed sincere. Sincere about what, I didn't know, but sincere nonetheless.

"I need you to find a good home for my cat."

I took off my glasses and rubbed my eyes. "Mr. Vinsley, I don't handle animal adoptions. I deal with animal behavior. I can give you the names of some wonderful people I know who—"

"No," he interrupted. "I specifically want *you* to find him a home."

"Why me?"

"Miss Johnson, I've read your books, seen you on TV, and heard about the work you do. You really understand cats. My cat, Dancer, is all I have, and I want the very best for him. I'll pay you for all the time you spend searching."

I was confused. "Why do you need to find him another home?"

Mr. Vinsley looked at me. I saw his eyes get misty for just a moment, and then he regained his composure. "Mr. Vinsley, are you all right?" I asked.

"I have cancer," he said in almost a whisper. He then went on to explain his reason for calling me. His doctor had told him he had less than nine months to live. He was not afraid to die, he assured me. After all, he had lived a good seventy-seven years. He had every comfort, had never wanted for anything, and was willing to face the end of his life with dignity. All of his business was in order. He had no family and wanted the money from his estate to go to cancer research, children's charities, and several animal-welfare organizations.

"There's just one important thing left to do," Mr. Vinsley said sadly. "I need to take care of Dancer. I found him four years ago and we've been best friends ever since. I need you to find him a home while I'm still alive. I want to know for sure that he'll be getting the love and care he deserves. I'll provide for his medical and food expenses." He looked down at his hands and then at me. "I know anyone else would think I'm a foolish old man, worrying about some cat, but he's been by my side through these very tough last years. When I was too sick to get out of bed, Dancer stayed right with me. He's a wonderful friend, and I want to make sure he lives a good life without me."

I didn't know what to say. Mr. Vinsley stood up, breaking my awkward silence.

"I'll introduce you to Dancer." With that, he left the room.

It was then I realized I'd been holding my breath as he'd been talking. I hadn't been expecting anything like this.

A few minutes later Mr. Vinsley came back, holding a gray cat in his arms. Dancer was a tough-looking male cat who had obviously seen more than his share of fights before becoming a resident at the Vinsley home. He was a huge cat, not fat, but tall and large. Both ears were torn at the tips and his nose bore several old scars.

Despite his rough exterior, Dancer's personality was sweet and gentle. Wrapped in his owner's arms, his loud purr sounded like an old car engine. Mr. Vinsley placed him on the floor, and the cat walked right over to greet me. Not content with just being petted, Dancer jumped into my lap and nuzzled me with his face.

Mr. Vinsley had found Dancer sitting on his car one cold winter morning. Having no fondness for cats at all, he promptly chased Dancer off the car, and that was that. Or so Mr. Vinsley thought. Every morning for the next week, there was this gray cat sitting on the roof of his beautiful Mercedes.

One morning as Mr. Vinsley watched the news on TV from his bed, he heard that the temperature would continue to drop during the day. It would be frigid by evening. Even though he didn't like cats, he hated the thought that the poor creature might freeze outside. Surely he must belong to someone. Mr. Vinsley planned on telling the owner of the cat to keep him on his own property. Perhaps he has a collar, Mr. Vinsley thought. So he quickly dressed and went out, fully expecting to find the big gray cat lounging on his car as usual. He opened the front door, felt the blast of cold air, and looked out. No cat.

Mr. Vinsley had never liked animals, and yet he found himself checking outside every few minutes, waiting for the cat. He kept telling himself that all he wanted to do was to find the owner of this pesky feline.

When the housekeeper arrived home from her morning shopping, she found Mr. Vinsley in the kitchen in his robe, spooning tuna into a dish. She didn't ask him what he was doing. He hadn't been eating well lately, so if he wanted to eat tuna at seven in the morning, why bother him?

Mr. Vinsley hurried outside and placed the dish of tuna on the roof of his car; then went back to his warm house to wait. His plan was to take the cat to the local shelter if it had no identification. He'd be rid of that stray one way or the other.

A widower for twenty-five years, Mr. Vinsley had also outlived his only son. With no grandchildren and no surviving relatives, he was very used to a life of solitude. He spent his days reading, listening to music, and walking around the beautiful grounds surrounding his house. He was comfortable being alone and was not at all interested in making friends or engaging in silly chatter with neighbors. His housekeeper jokingly referred to him as "Scrooge."

By the end of the day, the tuna, now quite frozen, was removed from the car. The housekeeper watched but knew better than to say anything.

"Have it your way, you stupid cat," Mr. Vinsley said as he went back inside the house and dumped the can in the garbage. Just before going to bed that night, he stuck his head out the front door one more time to check for the annoying cat. He wasn't out there, so Mr. Vinsley locked the door and went to bed.

At about 2:00 A.M., Mr. Vinsley woke up. He swears it was a terrible thirst that drove him out of bed and down the stairs to the kitchen. Along the way, he stopped for a quick peek out the front door—still no cat sitting on the car. But just as Mr. Vinsley was about to close the door he caught sight of something limping toward him. Hobbling up the driveway was the gray cat. His fur was matted and his right front paw dangled helplessly in the air. Mr. Vinsley stepped out onto the porch, but as soon as he did, the gray cat stopped.

"I'm not going to hurt you," he said to the cat. "Come here and I'll help you."

The cat just looked at him, not moving. Mr. Vinsley didn't know if he should go in to get more food. What if the cat ran off? But he knew he had to do something soon—the cold air was going right through his thin robe.

Leaving the front door open, he slowly stepped into the house and padded into the kitchen, where he dumped some leftover chicken onto a large plate. He was afraid the cat would be gone, but when he got back to the front porch, there the cat was, standing in the driveway with his paw in the air.

Mr. Vinsley placed the food on the porch and leaned against the doorway. The old man and the cat just looked at each other.

Mr. Vinsley really hadn't cared about anybody in a long time, and he didn't know why he was so concerned about this cat now. There was just something about him. Yet here were these two tough old guys, so used to being alone that they didn't even know how to ask for help.

"I generally don't care for your kind, you know," Mr. Vinsley said to the hesitant feline. "But, please, let me help you. Come on, it's too cold for me to be out here."

A few minutes passed. Mr. Vinsley was shivering. The cat was watching him intently; he seemed to be making a decision.

The old gray cat limped up to the porch, sniffed at the plate of food, then weakly hobbled past it and through the open doorway.

Amazed that the cat had voluntarily walked into the house, Mr. Vinsley followed him in and closed the door. "I don't blame you for passing up the chicken," he said to the cat. "Regina's not a very good cook."

After some hesitation, the cat allowed Mr. Vinsley to examine his injured paw. It would need medical attention first thing in the morning. In the meantime, the scruffy old thing would spend the night in the kitchen. As Mr. Vinsley bent down to scoop him up, he darted off on his three good legs in the direction of the stairs. Before he could be stopped, he clumsily hobbled up toward the bedrooms.

Planning to retrieve the nuisance cat in a moment, Mr. Vinsley went back to lock the front door. Cold and tired, he then climbed the stairs. Figuring that the frightened cat would be hiding under the beds, he switched on the light to begin his search. But the cat had already decided that being *on* the bed was much more comfortable. There he was, curled up at the foot of the huge bed.

"You could've at least chosen one of the guest rooms," Mr. Vinsley commented. But he was too tired to argue, so he crawled under the covers, stretched his feet out next to the cat, and turned out the light.

"Don't get too used to this. You're leaving in the morning."

The following morning, on the way to his own doctor's appointment, Mr. Vinsley dropped the cat off at the nearest veterinary hospital.

It was at this visit to the doctor that Mr. Vinsley learned he had cancer. Depressed and frightened, he drove home, almost forgetting to stop at the vet's. In fact, when he realized he was about to pass the animal hospital, he seriously considered just leaving the cat there for the vet to deal with. But he stopped anyway.

The gray cat had a broken leg. When the veterinary technician brought him out he was sporting a large splint. Mr. Vinsley paid the bill and left with the cat. Even though he didn't understand why, he felt a tug at his heart when he held the cat in his arms.

Three weeks into the new relationship, Mr. Vinsley's health took a serious turn for the worse and he was confined to his bed. The cat, by now named "Dancer" —because he could move so gracefully despite his heavy splint—left Mr. Vinsley's side only to use his litter box and grab a generous amount of food.

The friendship grew deeper and deeper. When Mr. Vinsley was well enough, the pair would stroll around the grounds or sit in the sun. Dancer loved to sleep in Mr. Vinsley's lap when he listened to classical music or read a book.

And another thing happened. Mr. Vinsley started chatting with neighbors about pets. They'd share stories and advice. After all these years, Mr. Vinsley was caring about others again. Soon his neighbors became friends who would often stop by for a cup of coffee or to play cards.

As I listened to Mr. Vinsley talk about Dancer, I promised myself I'd do everything I could to fulfill his wish.

I made several trips to visit Mr. Vinsley and Dancer. We'd have tea together and talk. I loved those afternoon visits and think of them often.

After a lengthy search, I found a potential home for Dancer—a sweet and gentle woman who had lost her husband years earlier. I thought it was a wonderful chance for Dancer to give this lonely person the same gift of love he'd given to Mr. Vinsley.

When Ruth Leeson met Mr. Vinsley and Dancer, all three of them hit it off. They spent much time together, and Mr. Vinsley took great pleasure in telling Ruth all about Dancer's likes and dislikes.

Eight months after I first met Mr. Vinsley, he was taken to the hospital. His housekeeper phoned to tell me that Mr. Vinsley wanted me to come get Dancer and take him to his new home. I canceled my appointments for the day, then called Ruth to tell her to expect Dancer.

I drove to the Vinsley residence. The housekeeper let me in and I collected Dancer's things. As if he knew what was about to happen, Dancer was waiting for me in Mr. Vinsley's room. He sat quietly on the bed.

The housekeeper walked me to my car. She touched my arm and thanked me for helping Mr. Vinsley. There were tears in her eyes. She'd worked for him for fifteen years.

Later that day I visited Mr. Vinsley in the hospital to tell him that Dancer was in his new home and that Ruth was doing everything she could to make him feel at home. He smiled. We talked a little while longer and then he drifted off to sleep. I quietly got up and stood by the bed for a few moments. "I'll keep watch over Dancer for you," I whispered, and left him to rest.

Two days later Mr. Vinsley died.

I've since visited Dancer in his new home several times, and he's very happy. He follows Ruth the same way he did Mr. Vinsley. And I've noticed that Ruth looks much more content than when I first met her. She proudly told me that Dancer sleeps on his own pillow next to her in bed.

Dancer, the once scruffy, tough stray cat, taught Mr. Vinsley how to love again. And now, the furry gray teacher with torn ears and a purr like an old car engine is helping Ruth to learn that same lesson.

—*Pam Johnson*

Blanche the Cat

Blanche the Cat did not get her name from her snow white coat, but because, like Tennessee Williams's heroine, she had "always depended on the kindness of strangers." She always welcomed people—big or little, loud or quiet, quick or slow people—to our home. She'd appear in front of them after they'd sat down, present her head expectantly for petting, and silently convey, "I'll be your friend if you'll be mine." People loved Blanche because they all got the same feeling from her—that she liked them better than anyone else.

We were living in North Carolina when we met Blanche. She lived in the house next door. The two fellows who lived there would leave town for days on end, leaving Blanche to stare out the kitchen window into our dining room window. I learned how to jimmy their back door to get in and leave extra food for her. One day, they announced they were leaving town for good. We asked for the cat and received her with thanks. She was about six months old, weighed six pounds, and was pregnant. This was in 1977.

We had always been cat people, my wife and I, since we married in 1971 right out of college. We'd had some memorable companions while living in Virginia, Connecticut, and Georgia. Right away, we took to Blanche because she was—pardon the expression—an underdog. Small and with a pronounced overbite and a thin tail, she was nobody's show cat. But her face was sweet and her temperament loving and gentle. She had learned from her former situation how to be patient in all situations. And above all, she had a special quality that we would later come to recognize as wisdom.

I'll go on for a minute about the wisdom. When she lived with us, Blanche always shared the house with other cats. I'll only go into the last two—Al the young ex-tomcat, and Gloria the neurotic fat cat. They're Blanche's feline family survivors. Blanche lived with Gloria for five years and with Al the last two. Gloria and Al have different objectives. Gloria wants to be the top cat, preferably an only cat. Al wants to have fun— preferably with Gloria, to whom fun is largely a foreign concept. Blanche was in the middle, between them.

In this triad, everyone agreed that Blanche, although the smallest, oldest, and weakest, held the moral high ground on the basis of seniority as well as on the basis of our obvious strong feelings for her. Resentful, Gloria would hiss and swipe at her occasionally and once lay on her and tried to crush her. Al would chase her at about three-quarter speed, which he knew was all she could muster. Here was one area where Blanche's wisdom shone—in her ability to accommodate her younger rivals. She never refused Al an invigorating chase, even when her bones ached so badly it would take her five minutes to lie down completely. And she never held Gloria's peevishness against her, but would curl up against her antagonist's hindquarters only minutes after Gloria had perpetrated some outrage against her.

Blanche trusted most people, but especially trusted me. Sometimes I would give her a ride, holding her high over my head and walking around the house. Other cats might have stiffened and bolted, but Blanche enjoyed the ride because of her trust that if she fell, I would catch her. There was a contract between us that neither of us would ever let the other down.

I scattered Blanche the Cat's ashes in a Shenandoah County, Virginia, field last Sunday. This field is the site of a house my wife and I have built for our retirement. It has a magnificent eastern view of Massanutten Mountain and of the valley between our house and the mountain. Blanche had never been there, but I've heard it said that the dead should have the best view, because they're dead so long. Blanche lived with us in the Washington, D.C., suburbs. I decided not to leave her ashes there because someday we would leave that house, and her, forever. We'll always be together in the valley. Now, when I look over Massanutten, I almost feel like I can see her face. I like to think of her as being in a place where there's always a sunbeam to warm her bones, and where she catches every field mouse she leaps for. Blanche was nineteen.

—*Anonymous from the Virtual Pet Cemetery*

The Prophet's Cat

Muhammad, the prophet who founded Islam, had great devotion and love for his cat Muezza. The prophet spoke often to his followers about the purity of the cat and the impurity of the dog. Because the cat possessed the Baraka, or blessing, it was always cherished by Muhammad's followers.

Muhammad's young acolyte Javad well understood the usefulness of the cat in keeping the granaries clean. Javad accepted in his heart the teaching of his master about how the cat came to be: when the Ark was over-run by mice, Noah passed his hand over the lion's head three times and the lion sneezed forth a cat that kept the mice in check. But Javad had trouble understanding how Muhammad could keep in his heart a love for a cat that seemed equal to the master's love for human be-ings.

One day, Muhammad's favorite cat, Muezza, fell asleep on his master's gellaba, or robe. When it came time for Muhammad to go to prayer, Javad awakened him. Muhammad rose onto his side and, saying not a word, carefully cut off the sleeve rather than disturb the cat's sleep. This was a story repeated many times with awe by Javad. Thus did the prophet teach him to open his heart to love and respect for all living things according to the will of Allah.

—Author Unknown

Sizi, Mon Petit Chat

Dr. Albert Schweitzer, the great humanitarian who won the Nobel Peace Prize in 1952, made his first trip to Africa in 1913 and eventually established a hospital in what was then the Belgian Congo. While his love for living creatures extended to his keeping of the thirty-fifth commandment of the Taoist monks of China—Thou shalt not intentionally crush insects and ants with thy foot—animals were neither equal to him nor the same. Each had its distinct role in the complex web of creation.

A special role in the doctor's life, a privileged place, was reserved for the cat.

Since no animal can be wantonly killed at the Lambarene Hospital, in the courtyard domestic animals wander freely about: hens and chickens, geese, goats and African sheep, dogs and cats. Monkeys scamper among the trees or on the corrugated roofs. The air is filled with the unmusical chatter of the weaver birds, busily stripping the fiber from the palm trees to make their spherical hanging nests. A white owl may be sitting under the piazza roof, or a pelican above the doctor's door, or a stork on the ridge pole. A porcupine is lumbering around the yard; a wild pig rooting about, its hungry eyes on the chickens. Among them all the doctor moves, with kindly, observing eye and generous hand, stopping to feed bits of meat to the white owl, or peel an orange for the antelopes, talk to the pelican, or smile at some chimpanzee's comical prank. At his heels are usually his dogs, splashed with the methylene blue that is used to combat the prevalent skin diseases.

There are insects humming everywhere. There is the story of the beetle that had been eating holes in the waterproof coat of a young visitor, ruining it. When the beetle fell out of the coat, the young man started to step on it, whereupon he felt a hand on his shoulder and heard the doctor say: "Gently, Noel! Remember you are a guest in its country."

At 6:00 every evening, when the bells of the Catholic mission on the island in the stream begin to toll, a pelican flaps its great wings, departs from his day's fishing, and takes his place on a high trellis gate in the courtyard. "Bon soir, Monsier le Pelican!" the doctor calls out. The pelican is the night watchman, who lets no one else pass up the steps except Mlle. Emma, who has a room in the house, and the doctor. Anyone else gets a powerful rap on the head. The doctor often has to pay the innocent in atonement for the pelican's hostility.

The only animal permitted to follow the doctor into the dining room is his dog, Tchu-tchu. A tiny beagle-type dog, she sits behind the chair and daintily receives morsels from his hand.

At night, when the doctor sits at the table in the pharmacy writing prescriptions, when he is alone, a time of quietude and reflection, the animal who sits on the table keeping him company is Sizi, his cat.

Sizi's mother disappeared when she was a kitten. The doctor fed her by hand with a medicine dropper and saved her life. Every afternoon at 2:30, Sizi comes to the doctor's room to be fed. She is a tiny cat, no wider than the doctor's forearm, with the appearance of a kitten who has never grown up.

In the evening, when the doctor is writing, Sizi often falls asleep on his left arm. The doctor continues to write with his right hand, but he will not move his left arm while the cat is asleep on it.

—*Charles R. Joy*

Minky Sue

She was the most beautiful black Siamese girl you've ever seen. (Well, her mother was a Siamese—her father, alas, was unknown.) Most *un*catlike, in that she loved new people and cuddling, and from day one, slept in the "Minky Spot" between my and my husband's pillow every night. When I lay down, I'd say: "Will you sing Mommy a Minky Song, so I can get to sleep?" And she did—with the loudest, most beautiful purr in the world.

We met when I went to a vacuum cleaner store one July day to get bags for my vacuum. Minky and a sister were there; and the moment she saw me, she threw herself into my arms and said: "Get me *out* of here!" I found out from the owner that a Siamese cat had two kittens on his lawn in May and never came back to them. Who knows why? I prefer not to imagine. The owner said I could take her, so I did—the fact that I had five others at home didn't seem to matter at all—to me or to Minky. She established her "Minky Spot" instantly, and for the next ten years, we were in separable. And always, every night, she would sing me to sleep.

In 1995, she came down with hepatic lippodosis (fatty liver) and went down to only about five pounds. We fought it, and she never complained when I had to force-feed her from a large syringe. She won that one, and I thought we would have many more happy years together; but it wasn't to be. Fibrosarcoma is a nasty, virulent form of cancer; and though Minky fought bravely through two operations, it turned out to be bigger than all of us. She never stopped loving me, and she never stopped singing me to sleep. Finally, on February 4, 1997, she was in a lot of pain and I knew that the time had come to let her go in peace. She sang her last Minky Song in my arms, at the doctor's office, at 7:45 that night. I promised her that she would never have to be in pain, and I kept that promise.

I have no one to sing me to sleep now. I don't sleep very well anymore. I will always have the wonderful memory of Minky, cuddled up in the Minky Spot, singing me to sleep with a Minky Song. This little girl is truly irreplaceable and will never be forgotten.

—*Anonymous from the Virtual Pet Cemetery*

My Pretty Lady

Do not tell me that cats never love people, that only places have real hold upon their affections. The Pretty Lady was contented wherever I went with her, and her attitude was always "wheresoever thou goest I will go, and thy people shall be my people."

She was fond of all the family. When we lived in Boston, whenever any of us came in the front door, she knew it. The Pretty Lady used to rouse from her nap in a big chair or from the top of a folding bed, jump down, and be at the hall door ready to greet the incomer. The cat never got down for the wrong person, and she never neglected to meet any and every member of our family who might be entering.

One summer we all went up to the farm in northern

Vermont and decided to take her and her son, Mr. Mc-Ginty, with us. On the farm the Pretty Lady seemed contented as long as I remained with her.

She was at first afraid of the big outdoors. The wide, windblown spaces, the broad, sunshiny sky, the silence and the roominess of it all were quite different from her suburban experiences; and the farm animals, too, were in her opinion curiously dangerous objects. Big Dan, the horse, was a truly horrible creature; the rooster was a new and suspicious species of biped; and the bleating calves, objects of her direst hatred. The pig in his pen possessed for her the most horrid fascination. Again and again she would steal out and place herself where she could see that dreadful, strange, pink, fat creature inside his own quarters. She would fix her round eyes widely upon him in blended fear and fascination. If the pig uttered the characteristic grunt of his race, the Pretty Lady at first ran swiftly away; but afterward she used to turn and gaze anxiously at us as if to say: "Do you hear that? Isn't this a truly horrible creature?"

Mr. McGinty made friends with every animal in the place and so endeared himself to the owners that he lived out his days there with a hundred acres and more as his own happy hunting ground.

Not so, the Pretty Lady. I went away on a short visit after a few weeks, leaving her behind. From the moment of my disappearance she was uneasy and unhappy. On the fifth day she disappeared. When I returned and didn't find her, I am not ashamed to say that I hunted and called her everywhere. I even shed a few tears when days rolled into weeks and she did not appear, as I realized that she might be starving or have suffered tortures from some larger animal.

There are many remarkable stories of cats who find their way home across almost impossible roads and enormous distances. There is a saying, believed by many people, "You can't lose a cat," that can be proved by hundreds of remarkable returns. But the Pretty Lady had absolutely no sense of locality.

She had always lived indoors and had never been allowed to roam the neighborhood. It was five weeks before we found trace of her, and then only by accident.

My sister was passing a field of grain and caught a glimpse of a small creature that she at first thought to be a woodchuck. She turned and looked at it and called "Pussy, pussy," when with a heartbreaking little cry of utter delight and surprise, our beloved cat came toward her. From the first, the wide expanse of the country had confused her; she had evidently lost her bearings and was probably all the time within fifteen minutes' walk of the farmhouse.

When found, she was only a shadow of herself, and for the first and only time in her life we could count her ribs. She was wild with delight and clung to my sister's arms as though fearing to lose her; and in all the fuss that was made over her return, no human being could have showed more affection, or more satisfaction at finding her old friends again.

That she really was lost and had no sense of locality to guide her home was proven by her conduct after she returned to her Boston home. I had preceded my sister and was at the theater on the evening when she arrived with the Pretty Lady. The latter was carried into the kitchen, taken from her basket, and fed. Then, instead of going around the house and settling herself in her old home, she went into the front hall, which she had left four months before, and seated herself on the spot where she always watched and waited when I was out. When I came home at eleven, I saw through the screen

door "that what was lost is found." She had been waiting to welcome me for three hours.

I wish those people who believe cats have no affection for people could have seen her then. She would
not leave me for an instant and manifested her love in
every possible way; and when I retired for the night,
she curled up on my pillow and purred herself contentedly to sleep, only rising when I did.

After breakfast that first morning after her return,
she asked to be let out of the back door, and made me
understand that I must go with her. I did so, and she
explored every part of the backyard, entreating me in
the same way she called her kittens to keep close by
her. She investigated our own premises thoroughly and
then crept carefully under the fences on either side into
the neighbor's precincts where she had formerly visited
in friendly fashion; then she came timidly back, all the
time keeping watch that she did not lose me.

Having finished her tour of inspection, she went in
and led me on an investigating trip all through the
house, smelling every corner and baseboard and insisting that every closet door should be opened, so that she
might smell each closet through in the same way.
When this was done, she settled herself in one of her
old nooks for a nap and allowed me to leave.

But never again did she go out of sight of the house.
For more than a year she would not go even into a
neighbor's yard; and when she finally decided that it
might be safe to crawl under the fences on to other
territory, she invariably turned about to sit facing the
house, as though living up to a firm determination
never to lose sight of it again. This practice she kept up
until the close of her last mortal sickness, when she
crawled into a dark place under a neighboring barn and
said good-bye to earthly fears and worries forever.

Requiescat in pace, my Pretty Lady. I wish all your sex

had your gentle dignity, and grace, and beauty, to say nothing of your faithfulness and affection. Like Mother Michel's "Monmouth," it may be said of you:

She was merely a cat,
But her Sublime Virtues place her on a level with
The Most Celebrated Mortals,
And
In Ancient Egypt
Altars would have been Erected to her
Memory.

—Helen M. Winslow; in 1900

CHAPTER TWO

Learning and Growing

Cat eyes seem a bridge to a world beyond the one we know.

Lynn Hollyn

The Mouser-Cat

Girls need women. Students need teachers. Apprentices need masters. Acorns need the shade and richness of the oak grove. A heart needs empathy. Everyone needs someone to shelter and protect them, to give them the courage to pursue their dreams, to not be afraid, to summon the will to *be* what they were meant to become.

Who would have guessed my teacher, my master, my mentor from girl to woman would be Mouser, my beloved Mouser-Cat?

I was a young girl when the Mouser came into my life; the Mouser, who would prove wise beyond her years, was then only a tiny kitten. Dad let the Mouser into my life on one condition: She would live in the barn to take care of the mice who came in to steal the horse's grain. But when I brought the tiny black-and-white kitten home from the shelter, my dad, with whom Mouser must have been sharing some of her wisdom already, said, "You can't put that little thing out in the barn. She'll freeze to death."

So we compromised: The kitten lived in my bedroom, and we called her "Mouser," nicknamed "The Mouser-Cat," to keep Dad happy.

Mouser, I think, knew our great expectations for her and became the most aggressive mousing cat ever known to humankind except . . . well . . . she seemed to think it was her duty to rid the world not of threats to the horse's grain, but to me.

Mouser, alas, had trouble distinguishing mice from dogs that came near me. It was dogs that she viciously chased from the house (even the ones who lived in it!), dogs she lay in ambush for in the front yard, howling dogs, screaming for their lives, she chased down the street, with me running after her.

"You've got to do something about that cat," Mom warned me. "She's terrorizing the neighborhood."

But I didn't do anything about that cat because I *couldn't*. Mouser made it clear from the beginning that it was *me* who belonged to *her*. She was terribly possessive of me. I think, in her catlike wisdom, she understood my fears of the big, wide world. And protect me she did!

Raise your voice at me and she would raise hers at you. She was very serious about protecting what belonged to her—and if her voice couldn't convince you of her intent, her claws would.

When my car was stolen, along with my house keys, a locksmith was called to change the door locks to my apartment. I got an urgent call at work, "You're going to have to come down here after all, Ma'am," he said kindly. "Your cat won't let me in the apartment."

When Mouser wasn't protecting me, she was equally assertive meeting her own needs. Mouser, you see, got everything she wanted from me, her best friend, including two meals a day. Mouser seldom failed to remind me that meals were to be served every morning and every night; and when she did fail to remind me, I'd sneak off to work or off to sleep, hoping she would never remember—because Mouser could stand to lose a few pounds.

One night, I'd been in bed for a good half hour when a horrible cat cry at bedside awoke me. I snapped on the night lamp and leaned over the mattress. Mouser was sitting there, blinking up at me with that "You thought I'd forget again, didn't you?" expression while a can of Fancy Feast sat nestled on the carpet between her front paws. She'd carried it in from the kitchen.

But as determined as Mouser was at voicing her own

opinion, she was equally affectionate—with me, that is, her possession. I would lie on the sofa, tap the center of my chest, and say, "Kiss? Kiss?"; and she would oblige me, leap onto my chest, press her forehead against my lips, and take as many kisses as a cat could stand. "The things some animals have to endure," she seemed to be saying, "just to get fed."

Mouser wasn't afraid of anything, even death. After thirteen years, the veterinarian told me what I'd feared most: She thought Mouser's kidneys and liver were cancerous. If exploratory surgery proved her worst suspicions, she asked me, "Should we let her go? Or should we bring her out of anesthesia to give us one more week, or one more day, or even one more moment, to say good-bye again?"

My answer caught in my throat. It was a question I couldn't even face. If Mouser left me, my heart would break. My life would never be the same without her. She had been my best friend since I was a young girl.

The night before her surgery, we were lying together on the cool kitchen floor. There was a dying light in her gaze that was fixed on the wall beyond me. She had lost so much weight she was merely a skeleton, and she hadn't eaten in days. I couldn't force one more pill down her throat. I wept with guilt when she fought me —as if she *wanted* to die and I wouldn't let her.

And I was weeping that night, lying on the floor with her, asking her with anguish in the hope she would understand: "What should I do, Mouser? Do you want me to let you go?"

As we lay there, only my crying audible, a flash of light came into Mouser's eyes. She turned her head in my direction and met my gaze. For a long minute that I had wished would be an eternity, she looked at me, almost through me. My eyes filled with tears and hers with an unexplainable smile.

"What?" I begged her silently. "Do you have the answer?"

She was only a few inches from my face; she pressed her forehead to my lips and asked me for a kiss.

"Do what is best for me," I believe she said. "I can accept life better than you can; after all these long, full years, I can accept death as well. In the end, doing what's best for me will bring peace to both our lives."

In the dying light of her eyes I felt Mouser was telling me: do not be afraid. Of life, or death. Or anything in between.

So the next day I did what Mouser had asked for in her kiss.

The kiss good-bye.

"Yes," I told the doctor finally of my decision. "Let her go."

I grieved and cried for many weeks for Mouser, my best friend. And if there is a lesson to this grief, it would be this, I must tell you: It is not an intangible thing we are removing from our midst when we kill the millions of dogs and cats every year in animal shelters across the country. It isn't a single ID number or a solitary statistic that dies when the light in a single cat's eyes dies. When we kill a million dogs and cats, we're killing a million lives who could touch us and heal us and bring us a kind of joy and warmth and peace in ways our fellow humans cannot. We're robbing a million beings of a million rays of sunlight, a million memories, a million heartbeats, a million lights of life.

We're killing a million Mousers.

And it was Mouser, after all, who taught me: Boldness has more to offer than fear. Life has more to offer than death.

That shelter kitten is waiting for you. *Go.*

—*Laura A. Moretti*

Tigger and the Touch

One of my early memories is that of standing in our family kitchen near Gibbons, Alberta, Canada, in the dawn light and hearing my grandfather's rabbit go thumping up the stairs to wake him. Every morning it was the same thing—the rabbit would hop up on the bed and rummage around under my grandfather's beard until he finally opened his eyes. "All right, all right," Grandpa would say grumpily.

I also remember my mother very firmly forbidding the cat to catch any mice in the house; and I remember, too, that very same cat having kittens and generously mothering a brood of ducks right along with her own litter. My father had come in from the hayfield one day and produced several duck eggs from the pockets of his jacket. Quickly, my mother slipped them in under the cat who was dreaming warm maternal dreams curled in her basket with her newborns.

After several days, a clutch of wispy ducklings emerged, adding yet another ingredient to the mix of kids, cats, dogs, and birds already whirling around in the big clapboard house with the green shutters.

In those early days on the farm, animals not only were members of the family and characters in their own right but were also such a natural part of life that a world without their everyday presence was unimaginable. My horse Trixie was not only my companion but also my only means of transport, taking me on the five-mile round-trip to school through the wintry Canadian snows and the mud and greening farmlands of spring. Life with the animals was an unself-conscious web of mutual support, survival, and pleasure. It was only later, when I moved out into the world, that I realized how far we humans have come from that connectedness. It seemed to me that we were distancing ourselves with increasingly dangerous results from our common bond with other species, from our old intuitive recognition that we are one with our fellow creatures, the same stuff of life, cell by cell, molecule by molecule.

Not until I was thirty-six years old did it finally dawn on me—after the end of a marriage, after twenty-five years of being captivated by horses, riding, showing, training, researching them, writing articles and books about them—that what I truly wanted was to somehow open people to a deeper connection with animals and to their tremendous importance in our lives.

A stray cat helped me make that discovery, helped me hear the calling that would change my life.

For me, discovery is like a marvelous puzzle. First there are only a few pieces of information and then gradually more and more appear until suddenly a picture begins to emerge. The pieces come together when I let my intuition guide me, that insistent little inner voice that speaks the truth and at the same time is so hard to trust.

Many years ago I read that intuition is *unlearned knowledge*, and that still makes sense to me. It's difficult, however, in our rationally oriented culture, to put faith in insights that whisper from inside ourselves or to trust as true and reliable inner knowledge that we arrive at inexplicably.

"How can I trust something that's just a feeling?" we say uneasily.

That was the voice I heard when I was thirty-six.

Every morning I stepped out to a beautiful view of oak-covered foothills rising in steep waves to the Sierra Nevada Mountains. Fascinating people from all over the world came to visit us at the Pacific Coast Equestrian Research Farm in Badger, California. I had a wonderful staff and caring friends. Outwardly, it was a perfect life.

Yet over a period of time my inner voice said, Is this what I was born for?

By following that inner voice I learned what was calling me—to develop a way of touching and communicating with animals I later called the Tellington Touch, or T-Touch, a type of intuitive *listening* with your hands that was impossible to describe.

One day at a clinic, a woman standing beside her horse said to me in frustration, "But Linda, just exactly what am I supposed to *do* with my hands?"

"Just push the skin in a circle anywhere on the horse's body," I told her, "and breathe into the circles as you make them." It was something that came out quite spontaneously, without thought; but it turned out the little circles allowed her to focus both her own and the horse's attention at the same time, and in a way that brought a deep sense of communion.

And so, almost unnoticed, the solution of my problem had appeared, the circular touch that was to be the foundation of the T-Touch—the circle, ancient symbol for life unending, for renewal, community, wholeness, and self.

The first cat I tried the T-Touch on was a stray. He was a tiger tom with wonderful, big jowls, extra-large paws, and a husky, strong body. I just loved him. He, on the other hand, cared only for breakfast.

Those who don't like felines often say that cats don't care about you. Millions of bedazzled cat owners, veterinarians, and psychologists will attest to the fact that this is simply not true. In my own parade of cats there have been many whose concern and sympathy for me bordered on the maternal.

Cats, however, *are* an independent breed and some are inclined to remain on distant though not unfriendly terms with humans. Some people find that haughty aloofness attractive, but what most of us want from a cat is a cozy relationship full of warmth and affection.

I was living in the famous California resort town of Carmel, a place that always reminds me of villages in fairy tales: The houses look like Hansel and Gretel cottages, and tiny shops that serve tea and crumpets dot the streets. At the base of the six-block main street you can see the ocean, and at night the trees on this boulevard are lit with hundreds of little lights, like fireflies.

The residential streets have no streetlights; they're dark at night and very quiet. I lived two blocks off the main street, and from my house I could take a dirt road down to the beach and the ocean or walk for miles on the many paths that crisscrossed the nearby forest.

Every morning, at seven o'clock sharp, the big tiger tom would appear at my door and ask to be let into the kitchen for breakfast. He'd march in, eat, and leave, very aloof, not interested in being petted and certainly not about to allow himself to be picked up.

I was away often then, sometimes for months, traveling around the world teaching; yet on the very day of my return, there he'd be at his post by the kitchen door, meowing for his breakfast as though he had received a telegram announcing that I was back. And then we'd start our old routine all over again.

One day as he was standing by the door licking his breakfast delicately off his whiskers and waiting to be let out, I thought to myself, This is really crazy. Why should I feed this cat all the time and not at least be able to hold him?

So I closed the door to the kitchen, and caught him— not an easy thing to do, I might add. I spent quite a few minutes following him around the room over and under chairs until I finally got hold of him. I restrained him on the table, not tightly enough for him to panic, but enough to keep him there for all of three minutes.

He didn't scratch or bite me, he just glared and struggled to get away.

I managed to get in a few fast circles all over his body. He didn't like it at all and stalked out the door looking ruffled, but he must have thought it over, because he showed up again the next morning and this time, when I repeated the procedure, he was much easier to restrain.

On the third day he sat quite still for large, very light Lying Leopard circles, closing his eyes until suddenly I was mindful of a different kind of awareness. Lying Leopard is the name I've given a gentle touch I use on sensitive animals when other touches may be too invasive or threatening. I also use it for fresh injuries to reduce the pain and the possibility of swelling. For this touch the leopard lies down, that is, the curve of the hand flattens somewhat, allowing a larger area of warm contact.

A quiet stream of nonverbal communication had begun to flow between us. It was very subtle, a heightened perception a little like that first moment of acuity when your ears pop open after pressure in an airplane.

Afterward he hung around for several hours.

On the fourth day he not only stayed for breakfast, he stayed for the rest of his life.

When faced with a nervous cat, the best way to introduce the T-Touch is by doing small circles all over the body, with a very light pressure. Push the fur in one-and-a-quarter-inch circles, clockwise, moving at random for the first few minutes. This focuses the animal's attention on you at the same time as it breaks the pattern of nervous reaction. And finally, because the animal can't anticipate, he or she very quickly gives up struggling. In subsequent sessions, slow the circles and connect them with a soft slide and a little pause between circles.

The wonderful thing about Tigger was how friendly he became. Later, after he became a close friend, I decided to move from Carmel to Naciemento, California. At first I had doubts about taking Tigger away from his home community and his daily round of backyards and forest hunting grounds. Perhaps it would be better to leave him with a friend in the neighborhood.

Tigger must have shared those same doubts.

When I loaded up the moving truck and pulled out for Naciemento, Tigger was nowhere to be seen. *He's hiding because he doesn't want to come along,* I thought sadly.

Fortunately, I made a second trip to get more of my belongings.

When the truck left for the second time, however, Tigger was still nowhere in sight.

After a third trip to Naciemento with the moving truck, I sadly resigned myself to Tigger's decision not to join me.

Finally, the moment came for me to lock up and leave my storybook house with the Dutch doors and the blooming garden. I went out to my car feeling bad about Tigger, whom I had seen briefly but who had disappeared shortly after breakfast.

As I stepped around to open the door on the driver's side, there he was, sitting pertly beside the front tire.

As soon as I opened the car door he brushed past me, hopped in, and looked at me as if to say, "Well, what are we waiting for? Let's go!"

He knew before I did that the time had come for him to declare his loyalty. My once-reclusive tiger tom had used his feline psychic abilities for more than simply knowing when to show up for breakfast.

Later, when I began running a retreat center and residential school for horsemanship in Naciemento, not only did Tigger sleep with me, he would make the rounds of the guest rooms and give each guest a visitation and a cuddle. He was a truly democratic cat and never left anybody out.

—*Linda Tellington-Jones*

Yoko's Gift

One summer afternoon, my two young daughters, seven and three, were having trouble sharing. The handing of possessions back and forth was eliciting screams of pain, howls, and tears. "Sharing seems so unfair!" my seven-year-old said, wise beyond her years. I tried to explain that sharing *is* unfair—at first—but that acts of kindness come back to you, in a circle. I tried to explain that you give because you believe in abundance—there will always be enough love for you, my sweet little daughter—not scarcity. I tried to explain that when she gave our big dog, Texas, a treat, he couldn't possibly give *her* a treat back. It was a one-way act of kindness. But at night, Texas refuses to come up to my bedroom, instead pushing open the downstairs door to be with Grace.

I told her that Texas would no doubt give his life to save her, if necessary—the ultimate act of sharing, of love.

My poor daughter burst into tears. "I don't want

Texas to die!" Oops. Words not so well chosen, Dad. A lesson for another day. Stories, not statements, make the best lessons anyway.

Someday I will tell her the story of Stephanie Laland, who writes cat books with a sense of humor and tenderness that few possess, and Stephanie's cat Yoko, and Yoko's gift.

One day Stephanie set about trying to find random acts of kindness practiced by cats, dogs, and other animals. She was inspired by the words of Anne Herbert, scrawled on a restaurant napkin in Sausalito, California, in 1982: "practice random acts of kindness and senseless acts of beauty." Anne's words became a battle cry of love that echoed around the world, a cry carried on bumper stickers and business cards and refrigerator doors and *Oprah*, leading to best-selling books and guerrilla acts of goodness everywhere.

Could animals be capable of the same moral sense as humans? Did they practice random acts of kindness and senseless acts of beauty?

Stephanie learned that Napoleon Bonaparte had wept only once on a battlefield—watching a dog who refused to leave the side of his dead master. Later, after falling overboard trying to escape exile in Elba, Napoleon was rescued by a Newfoundland.

Stephanie learned of a cat named Bill who stayed home while his human was away on a trip. But when the man was injured in a railway accident and died a few days later in a distant hospital, the man's brother was shocked to see Bill appear at the funeral in the hospital graveyard. The faithful cat sadly looked down upon the coffin, and began his long journey home.

She learned of an English miner who saw two rats walking along a road carrying a straw in their teeth together. In fear, the man killed one of the rats—and was astonished when the other rat, straw in its mouth, didn't attack him. Then he noticed the other rat was blind.

Stephanie learned that of the two thousand skeletons found at the volcanic destruction of Pompeii, one was of a dog. The inscription on the dog's collar told how he had saved his master, Severinus, three times—once from drowning, once from thieves, once from a wolf. The dog's skeleton was found stretched protectively over the bones of a boy, the son of Severinus.

She learned of Elsa, a blind woman in San Diego, who raised her cat, Rhubarb, to be a feline "Seeing Eye dog." When Elsa is outside and the telephone rings, Rhubarb comes and fetches her, guiding her into the house. (Concerned about Elsa's energy level, Rhubarb puts his paw on her leg to signal, "You've talked enough.")

Stephanie learned that animal mothers, both cats and rats, will endure any pain, any amount of electric shock, even death, to protect their young during scientific research.

She learned that Lincoln and Gandhi and Harriet Beecher Stowe and Pablo Casals and Shelley and President John Tyler were convinced that animals committed more random acts of kindness than humans ever could.

She learned that in Glasgow, Scotland, some hospices let cats stay with terminally ill patients. The cats lie quietly with the patients, lessening their fear of dying alone.

Eventually, Stephanie's research became a book: *Peaceful Kingdom: Random Acts of Kindness by Animals.* In one particularly moving passage, she wrote of a mongrel dog named Shep, who was not allowed to board the funeral train that carried his master's casket to a distant burial site from Fort Benton, Montana, in 1936. Inconsolable, Shep sat down on the railway platform and waited for his master's return—for five and a half years, until Shep himself died by the very tracks that had carried his master away.

She wrote of a dolphin who taught an autistic boy to better communicate and love both animals and people —and brought the boy's parents tears of gratitude and joy.

On the following page, Stephanie Laland wrote another story:

> At a very low point in her life, a woman saw no way out and decided to commit suicide. As she sat on her bed weeping and wondering what method to use, her cat jumped on her and began licking her tears away. Realizing that when another creature loves you there is always hope, the woman decided to live and ultimately went on to write this book.

Thank you, Yoko.

Stephanie's life was Yoko's gift. And so Stephanie's journey was a circle that began with an act of cat kindness and ended with a book full of love and kindness and simple gratitude—to the cat who started it all.

Someday, when she's old enough to understand, I'll tell Grace.

—*Michael Capuzzo*

My Checkered Past

I grew up in a simpler time in a simpler place than our world is now, on a seventy-five-acre farm with many animals. It's the cats I remember most.

When I was five, Calico peeked out of my dad's overcoat pocket one evening upon his return from work, and I stared back with wide, eager eyes. She taught me how to love and be loved in return.

When I was a young girl, I opened the door for a scrawny little stray who was begging to be part of our lives. Tigger called forth from me pity and compassion. Later, when he became big and strong and the mighty hunter of our farm, spurning the front door to enter and exit boldly through the windows, he showed me how exciting it was to grow and change.

Tigger's proudest moment came the day he caught his first field mouse, hopped up on his accustomed windowsill and tried to utter his loudest "Please let me in!" What a decision! A very loud meow would let the mouse escape and dash his hopes of displaying his hunting prowess. With quiet humility, he would have his mouse but no one would ever see it. Growing into a mighty hunter wasn't going to be easy!

Luckily for Tigger, my mother passed the window, praised him for his skill, but let him know the mouse was not welcome in the house.

Tigger could be a gentle friend, too. My mighty hunter let me tie a baby bonnet under his chin and wheel him around in my doll buggy.

When I left the farm and became a mother, I thought I had left my cats and the lessons of my childhood behind forever. I had a life to build and sons to raise and so many new challenges on my mind. But as my sons grew, they let me know that parakeets, rabbits, gerbils, and even a dog weren't enough. A cat had to be part of the family.

Blackie was a bold windowsill jumper. He never failed to appear on our neighbor's kitchen sill whenever the aroma of cooking liver assailed his pink nose.

Marmalade could be a fireball of energy when my youngest son wanted him to be. But he was happiest draped around my boy's neck as a huge yellow fur piece, both of them quietly content.

Now that I am almost seventy-five, I find myself remembering the farm in greater clarity, like an old painting I have returned to, seeing fresh strokes of color. It is Checkers who stands out in sharpest relief.

He was huge and sleek with a startling black-and-white fur coat. He shared my grandmother's home, and they were indeed two of a kind. Both were very independent but easy to love and admire. I think Checkers enjoyed as many privileges as we, her grandchildren, did. His upholstered chair in the living room was a sight to see. One side was almost totally destroyed—his claw sharpener! He shared her bed, but never until the room was dark. Then he would stretch himself out full length, back to back with his loving mistress. The house they shared was a restored nineteenth-century stone farmhouse with a rather unusual water system. The water was pumped by a hydraulic ram from a spring in the meadow to an enormous wooden storage tank in the attic. From there it ran by gravity to the kitchen and bathroom of my grandmother's house.

One night, my grandmother was awakened by Checkers's loud meowing beside her bed. After several admonishments did not succeed in silencing him, my grandmother followed him groggily into the hallway. Checkers ran immediately to the attic door, meowing loudly and pawing frantically at the door. Totally mystified and just a little annoyed, my grandmother opened the door and flipped the switch, flooding the attic steps with light. Just beginning to cascade down the steps was a very healthy stream of water, overflowing from the storage tank! A hasty call to my father, and the pump was shut off, preventing a disastrous flood. With crisis solved, Checkers sauntered back to the bedroom with his usual airy confidence, his detached mood indicating "It's all in a night's work." Ever after, I felt I should curtsy to him in deference to his uncanny knowledge of disaster looming on the horizon. Who knew what Checkers's next move would be?

When I sit at my typewriter, I try not to let Sparky, my amour of the moment, read this; and I silently mouth my apologies to all the other very intelligent and loving furry critters who have brightened my days. Sparky thinks she is the only feline who has ever shared my love and my life. She knows nothing of a ten-year-old girl who lived on a farm with many animals, and a cat named Checkers who taught her that life was a difficult challenge and a foreboding journey; but there was tenderness and courage and mystery and quiet bliss with our feline friends to share the way.

—*Marianna K. Tull*

The Halloween Gift

This may be the most mundane cat story you have ever heard. I am sorry if it is so, but writing this is a catharsis for me. I imagine many people have had a similar experience.

Baggins died, head cupped in my hand, one year ago Halloween morning. And though our fourteen-year relationship might have had many ordinary moments, he was the magical messenger who taught me even a plain domestic shorthair makes life extraordinary.

I was raised a true-blue canine fan. I conceded to cat ownership, when, as a single waitress in a city apartment, I wanted a pet more responsive than a fish but less routine-dependent than a dog. A co-worker had a one-year-old black-and-white male, a gift she'd never warmed up to, so I took him off her hands. I remember crying the first week because I thought his timid retreat under the bed meant he knew that I knew nothing about cats and feared he'd moved from a home of indifference to one of total incompetence.

But in time my tuxedo-patterned pal came out from under the bed and won me over with more endearing traits than I can name. He had not been weaned, for one, and suckled at my neck on a daily basis, kneading and purring and loving my terry cloth robe lapel to permanent discoloration. He knew my particular neck, too—on the rare occasion he found another, he'd realize his mistake just before the ritual commenced and back away with total fidelity. For some reason, despite normal feline distaste for water in general, Baggins loved to stick his head beneath the faucet as I brushed my teeth in the morning until he had nearly a puddle between his ears. When I pointed out to him that I needed to spit once finishing my teeth, he accommodated by leaping into the tub, waiting for me to turn on that spigot once again so he could continue his morning bath until I put my contact lenses in and all taps were shut off.

At about age eight, Baggins survived what the veterinarian told me was a hopeless case of kidney failure. We discovered then that only one of his kidneys worked anyway, the other apparently shriveled congenitally. He also thrived despite my delay in getting him to the vet since my lack of experience with cats helped me miss some subtle behavioral signs. So when my own illness disabled me from working in 1993, I thanked him for not leaving me alone when he'd had that chance to explore his next life. I asked him to see me through his eighteenth birthday, certain I would be back to work by then and more able to handle his inevitable departure. (I had some unrealistic ideas about cat longevity—the only two cats I did know as a kid lived to be twenty.)

My faithful friend waited, I am certain. He intentionally held on to those extra eight lives until one night in October. I came home that very day from a hospitalization myself. Despite the joy of our reunion, this time I knew by midnight something was wrong. At three in the morning we were at the emergency room of the veterinary hospital at the University of Pennsylvania in Philadelphia. There he stabilized, and I transferred him to my veterinarian's clinic, Baggins's previous place of healing. His vital signs returned, but not all of Baggins did. The vet suggested that even more familiar surroundings sometimes restored what medical attention could not. That was the last possible remedy for the appetite, motor strength, and sparkle he'd lost. So I took Baggins home.

You all know the outcome, don't you? You have owned cats and had to stop the silent pleading in your heart long enough to hear your gentle friend tell you how to thank him for sharing probably more of your life's moments with him than with most humans. He was there, suckling, wetting his head, and purring through myriad jobs, men, apartments, celebrations, vacations, and uncountable nights curled so sound asleep behind my knees that I would rather lie awake than disturb him. We spent that last weekend in seclusion together. He held on till Monday morning so there was no chance my sleepy eyes might miss his good-bye. And his last look was one of gratitude.

Then Baggins gave me the strangest, greatest gift. He taught me to grieve. That wrenching pain that tells you what an extraordinary chance you have had to love and be loved back. There was something simple and exquisite about mourning my cat. And that is what I told my new SPCA foundling, on Halloween day, the next year. I picked up Baggins's picture, showed it to this new funny feline, whose different but equally endearing idiosyncrasies gradually filled in empty, aching spaces. This one, Summit, likes heights, not sinks, and fetches but does not suckle. I said, "Summit, this is the guy who taught me the joys of cooing shamelessly over cats, and whose simple absence brought me desperately in search of you." And Summit put his nose to mine, licked a tear off my cheek and purred softly as I scratched him under the chin.

—*Bonnie L. Crouthamel*

Jasper

I'm sorry, boy, that
I ignored you that day.
I'm sorry that
I took your routine and cheerful greeting for granted
and
when you insisted on sitting on my
important
papers,
while purring loudly in my ear,
I got frustrated
and simply pushed you aside.

Your soft orange-and-white body rubbed beneath my
chin
but I did not have time for you, boy.

Nevertheless, you persisted.
Your purr grew louder
and I grew more annoyed.

I was busy, boy, with my
important
work.
I was much too busy for you.

You soon gave up
and went on with your business
and I went on with
mine.

I am sorry, boy, that I
did not understand
what you were doing
that day.

I turned my head,
not knowing,
that what you were trying to tell me
was

Good-bye.

—Anna Biggerstaff. Age 16

CHAPTER THREE

Hope and Perseverance

I will always remember the olive-eyed tabby who taught me that not all relationships are meant to last a lifetime. Sometimes, just an hour is enough to touch your heart.

Barbara L. Diamond

Near the book a notebook
near the notebook a glass
near the glass a child
in the child's hand a cat.
And far away stars stars.

Oktay Rifat, trans. Taner Baybars,
from the Turkish

A Mother's Love

The call came through at 6:06 on Friday, March 19. An abandoned warehouse in a run-down Brooklyn neighborhood was on fire. Thirty firefighters rushed to the scene through a driving early spring snowstorm. At the wheel of one of the six fire trucks was David Giannelli. In his seventeen years as a New York City firefighter, Giannelli had bravely entered hundreds of burning buildings conducting lifesaving search-and-rescue missions.

Heroism comes from someplace deep inside, from a reverence for life that summons the best from the human soul. But that day, the world would learn something new about David Giannelli's capacity as a hero, as his heroism took a different, perhaps rarer, form— that of keeping his eyes and his heart open, that of caring as much for another species as for his own.

Finding a new level of heroism would not be easy. "The whole place had gone up like a bonfire," said Giannelli. Giannelli and the other members of Brooklyn Ladder Company #175 were already familiar with the building from previous fire calls. They knew that there was no place inside the dilapidated structure where someone could have become trapped; but that if there were, by now the fire was raging so out of control any rescue attempt would have been foolhardy, if not impossible.

But then, near the end of fighting the fire, Giannelli heard three faint cries for help. He followed the anguished sounds, which led him to a trio of tiny stray kittens cowering against the outside wall of the next building over, not five feet from the flames. Their fur was scorched and smoky. They were all alone.

Giannelli found a box and moved the kittens farther

out of harm's way, then went back to help with the fire
hoses. But a few minutes later he heard more meows.
This time the source was harder to pinpoint, but after
several minutes of searching, Giannelli spotted two
more kittens huddled against another building—this
one across the street from the burning warehouse.
These kittens, too, were scorched from the flames.
They, too, had been left alone.

Ever so gently, Giannelli nestled them into the box
alongside their littermates. He knew there had to be a
mother cat somewhere nearby. Glancing over at the
smoldering embers of the warehouse, he murmured, "I
hope she got out in time."

While the rest of the fire crew stowed away their
equipment, David Giannelli spent some time searching
for the kittens' mother.

In an abandoned lot not far from where she'd left the
second two kittens, he found her, hiding behind a pile
of rubble.

She could have escaped the fire herself easily. But this
devoted mother cat had braved the inferno five times as
she carried her offspring one by one to safety. Then,
after ferrying two of them across the street to an even
safer place, she had collapsed on her way back for a
third.

"My heart dropped when I saw her," recalled Giannelli. "She wasn't moving at all, and at first glance, I
didn't even think she was breathing. Her mouth and
face were badly scorched, and the bottoms of her paws
were blistered and caked with soot. Her ear flaps and
whiskers were all but gone. Her fur was so burned,
there were large patches of skin showing through."

The cat emitted a whimper of pain as the fireman
lifted her up. "At least she's alive," he thought, and
carried her to the box so she could be reunited with her
litter.

Giannelli still marvels at what happened next.

"The kittens started mewing, all excited to see their mama. Only, their mama couldn't open her eyes to see them, her lids were so swollen from all the smoke and burn blisters."

And so the brave mother made do as best she could. Standing there amid her litter on legs wobbly from pain and exhaustion, she pressed her nose against each of the kittens in turn and sniffed—identifying and counting. One, two, three, four, five. Only after she'd completed the head count and satisfied herself that all five of her babies were present and accounted for did she allow herself to lie down inside the box. Arranging her scorched body protectively around her babies, she started purring a weary, guttural purr.

"It was the most incredible, the most heartwarming thing I've ever seen," said Giannelli.

Several years earlier, the modest firefighter risked life and limb to retrieve a puppy someone had left leashed to a post inside another abandoned building that had gone up in flames. After administering oxygen on the scene, Giannelli had carried the dog back to the firehouse, where he'd tried to find a shelter that would agree to help. He'd all but given up hope when he reached the North Shore Animal League, in Port Washington, Long Island. The league readily offered to treat the puppy's burns and subsequently went on to find him a good home.

David Giannelli needed to make only one phone call to enlist aid for his family of feline refugees. "Bring them to us immediately," a league employee instructed him. Forty minutes later when Giannelli pulled into the lot, he found the league's entire medical staff waiting outside in the blustery snowstorm.

Scarlett was a mass of raw burns, gasping for breath.

The kittens couldn't open their smoke-damaged eyes. The staff rushed the kittens into the facility's clinic, where they split into two teams led by Dr. Bonnie Brown, the league's medical director, and Dr. Larry Cohen, the assistant director. Dr. Brown took charge of the kittens, while Dr. Cohen treated their mother, whom a league employee quickly dubbed Scarlett because of all the patches of singed, reddened flesh. The mother cat and her kittens were all treated for shock, and their wounds were cleaned and dressed. They were given intravenous antibiotics to help stave off infections, after which they were placed inside a special intensive care animal cage where league veterinarians could keep a watchful eye on the oxygen levels, temperature, and humidity.

For a while it was touch and go with Scarlett and the tiniest of her four-week-old brood. Happily, however, both mother and kittens responded excellently to treatment. Saturday, when Dr. Cohen placed a dish of food in front of Scarlett, the cat wolfed it down ravenously, and soon she was back to nursing all five of her purring progeny. Three days passed before she managed to open her still-swollen eyes just a bit, but Scarlett regained her eyesight completely.

For three months they healed, though one kitten died. Scarlett's courage became an inspiration to people all over the world. The mother cat appeared on *Regis and Kathie Lee*, CNN, and *Good Morning, America*. Oprah's people begged to fly Scarlett out to Chicago for a Mother's Day appearance (Scarlett was still recovering from her wounds, so Oprah had to settle for footage).

In a media age that focuses on stories of loss, ineptitude and pain, Scarlett's power was simple and fundamental. Rosemary Asmussen captured it in a poem.

FROM A HEROINE
Why is everyone so surprised
That I saved my furry five;
That in spite of pain and danger
I brought them out alive?
True, my eyes were barely open
But I heard their frantic wails;
Through smoke and flames I saw
Scorched ears and burning tails.
Every trip was a burdened choice
But I could make no other
The rescuers have called me cat
But I am also "mother."

Scarlett found a home with Karen Wellen of Brooklyn, New York. Karen works in a coffeeshop and does freelance writing. The arrival of Scarlett brought her a joy she hadn't known, she said, since her own painful recovery from a car accident seven years earlier, during which her twenty-one-year-old cat died.

"The physical and emotional pain I have endured through these years have made me a more compassionate person," Karen said. "And I vowed that if I ever allow another cat to enter my life it would be one with special needs."

"I can't recall another case that even comes close to matching the outpouring of public support we've received in regard to Scarlett and her kittens," stated Marge Stein, manager of adoption services for the North Shore Animal League. "We're getting thousands of calls. We can't even keep up."

But the multitude may have to line up behind a certain firefighter who has been a frequent visitor to the convalescing cats. In the old myths, the stories emblazoned forever on the human heart, the hero cannot survive without a guardian, without a mentor to help show her the path. The strongest mentors or guardians are often heroes themselves, like David Giannelli, who know valor and its needs when they see it. On March 19, David Giannelli more than fulfilled his end of the bargain as a guardian for a hero cat and her little family. Some of our bravest heroes would stop there. But there is another role, a gentler role, needed for life, human and otherwise, to survive and thrive; and David Giannelli wanted that role, too.

Said Giannelli with a shy smile, "I've got my eye on one of these kittens."

—*Bill Holton and Michael Capuzzo*

The Gift

We lived in a large house, and my cat, Sammi, always took pride in leaving me small field mice at the door each morning. She was extremely proud of these successful hunting ventures and looked forward to my praise of these small gifts at the door. Then, we had to move to a very small apartment. There were no fields for her to play in, and only a few trees to climb.

When I finally let her out solo, she greeted me at the door the following morning as was her habit, talking up a storm and just as proud as she could be. When I looked down, there at my feet were two small pinecones. I was absolutely amazed. She continued to bring a pinecone or two to the door each morning until the day she died.

I will never forget Sammi. My little cat showed me that no matter what the situation, we can find a way to make the best of it. To this day, when things are hard to deal with, I see her at the door with those pinecones.

—Susan Huskins

Circle of Soft Light

Today is the first day of spring. The official first day. It is late afternoon and the wind is unrelenting. The tall evergreen outside the window where I write whips against the house like ropes, and I am thrown into such anguish. I fear everything. Foolish, foolish, very real fear. This morning for an hour, unexpected snow fell, thick quick flakes covering the trees and ground. Within minutes it disappeared. The sun came and went. Now this wind digs an empty space.

The cats have crawled into the back of the bookcase and pushed books all over the floor. Someone has chewed the corner off *Seeing with the Mind's Eye: The History, Techniques, and Uses of Visualization.* It is impossible to place blame. The resident group of cats currently living in these upstairs rooms is five, but can swell to a dozen or more during the day.

I strongly suspect Paula Carlene of the book damage. A tortoise cat with a face like a checkerboard, intelligent placid eyes, and a perfect tiny head placed on one of the largest cat bodies I have ever seen. She sleeps now, barely visible on my down comforter. Awake, she fancies paperback books. She eats them, not in secret but openly, with great chomping pleasure. I found her eleven years ago at the tail end of a hurricane, outside my hotel room in Florida, so tiny then I could almost hold her in one hand, visions of millions of meals dancing in her head. I ordered breakfast, and she ate it— scrambled eggs, buttered whole wheat toast, bacon, cream—stopping only at the juice and coffee.

I spent the morning trying to find out if she belonged to someone. It seems I have spent a major part of my life clutching one cat or another searching for a bereaved owner. All over the world, cats in my arms are met by a blank expression reserved for a madwoman. Have I ever found a grateful owner? I can't remember one. That particular wet morning no one spoke English, or perhaps no one wanted to, and certainly no one recognized this tiny kitten. So that afternoon I moved to the apartment that had been prepared for me with a new, unclaimed cat. I lived in that apartment complex for ten weeks, surrounded by young singles. I was able, without too much effort, to acquire eight cats in those ten weeks.

Days after settling in, along came a momma cat with two outrageously beautiful kittens; tiny, fine long-haired kittens, curly tufts of wispy fur peeking from their ears. I wondered how she had done it, this thin, ordinary, spotted black-and-white cat, and how inordinately proud she seemed. I caught them with a beach towel, one after the other. I struck quickly from the rear, soon after I had placed a large plate of food on the grass.

Once in the apartment, the kittens discovered the drapes. Their tiny feet rarely hit the floor. They hung suspended, swinging with pleasure, while their mother refused to come out from under the bed. The kittens occasionally joined her there for meals. Momma cat took all of hers under the bed until I hauled her out, howling, to be spayed.

On her return, she called a halt to the free meals but decided on a routine of cleanliness that bordered on madness. No one was spared; even Paula Carlene was pinned to the floor. Every inch was covered. Momma cat pursued them without mercy. They all took to the drapes. Paula's ever-increasing bulk causing large gaps in the fragile beige fabric. They were to be my second pair of floor-to-ceiling drapes replaced at some expense on my exit from a rented house.

Today, eleven years later, Momma cat lies on a box of old photos, her legs tucked under her against the wind, watching me as I sit writing. She's now a round gentle cat, simply called Momma. One of her daughters lives in my mother's room, an only cat except for nights when two orange toms are allowed in to sleep. She reigns queen. My mother claims she is a miniature cat and tells this to people who believe her, for she believes it herself. She is small, never having grown, in my opinion, either in body or mind. My mother disagrees, and she should know, for they live incestuously in the dark green room at the top of the stairs, watching television and smoking cigarettes. If I dare to go in, she rushes wildly about on short little legs while continually emitting a high-pitched squeak.

Once, a few years ago, my mother went on vacation, and I brought the cat down from the green room. It seemed to me she rather enjoyed being included. Per-

haps I read the signs wrong, for she had a kind of fit
and fell off the kitchen table and had to be rushed to
the vet. I returned her to the green room, and once
restored, she returned to herself.

My Florida cat family grew by four more one afternoon when I returned home to find a cardboard box
filled with kittens. Earlier that day I had made what I
considered an impassioned, eloquent plea for neutering
and spaying on a local TV interview show. Someone
was watching. I had positive proof: four kittens and a
note that read "Put your money where your mouth is."

That very evening, as I emptied my growing amount
of trash, I found a half-grown cat tied securely in a
heavy nylon laundry bag and deposited in the trash
container. He was the most magnificent of acquisitions,
a pale, creamy orange half-Siamese, lovely rough,
tough boy cat.

It is growing dark now, and I go downstairs to the
kitchen. Everywhere cats are gathering for evening
treats, sitting on counters, asleep in baskets, warming
themselves under lamps. A great mound of cats curl
together on the long kitchen table. Mary Frances is
asleep in a big blue-and-white mixing bowl. Bonnie has
torn up the front page of *The New York Times* and lies
content in a paper nest.

I sit alone with a glass of wine in this large white
kitchen filled with things I have collected, listening to
the gentle crunching of some forty cats eating tiny
multishaped bits of dry food. From the chair facing the
window I can see the perfect crack from top to bottom
in the yellow glass shade of my lamp, broken in a failed
flying leap from the top of the refrigerator to the yellow table. I must always remember that these cats care
not at all for my things—so many broken things over
the years—vases, plates, cups, lamps. The corners of
my soft pine chests are shredded, the rungs of chairs

like whittled sticks, and tables bear long scars of sliding cats.

I had a lovely, funny, fat cat called Octavia who used to back up and pee into the telephone jacks, causing a complete shutdown and labored explanations to the phone company. Last year the condenser in the refrigerator burned up. The repairman discovered abnormal amounts of cat hair that had collected and caught fire. Exclamations of horror and surprise seemed pointless. The man was standing in a kitchen filled with some thirty very interested cats, and they weren't bald.

I have a long, narrow table in the kitchen, painted years ago in bright yellow enamel. It has been with me a long time and bears many scars. It now sits under the window and is never empty. The cats watch the world through this window, and I watch with them. In this almost darkness, the yellow glass lamp creates a circle of soft light, and I can forget for a second all the fears I carry. In this early darkness there is a kind of momentary peace.

—Sandy Dennis

The Tribe of Tiger

The title of my book, *The Tribe of Tiger*, is from a poem called "Rejoice in the Lamb," written sometime between 1756 and 1763 by the English poet Christopher Smart. The poem is long and rambling to the point of incoherence, a product of the confusion the poet experienced and for which he was kept in solitary confinement in a madhouse. A more frightful setting than a rat-infested madhouse of the eighteenth century would be hard to imagine, as would the loneliness and despair that Smart must have known during his eight-year ordeal. His torment was mitigated, however, by the presence of a cat, Jeoffry, who became the subject of one section of the poem—some seventy-five radiant lines that are today well known and much beloved by cat fanciers and that often appear as a poem in their own right, usually under such titles as "Of His Cat, Jeoffry" or "Jeoffry" or "For Jeoffry, His Cat." The rest of the poem is virtually lost, known only to a handful of scholars of English literature.

My book is but one of dozens, perhaps even hundreds, of books about cats that take their titles from "Jeoffry." Almost anyone who reads the fragment, even those who are unaware of Smart's confinement and suffering, can share the strength of his feeling. In the following lines, for example, one feels the poet's prayerful gratitude for Jeoffry's company in the echoing asylum during the black, terrifying hours of night:

For I will consider my cat, Jeoffry.
For he is the servant of the Living God, duly and
   daily serving him.
For he keeps the Lord's watch in the night against
   the adversary.

For he counteracts the powers of darkness by his electrical skin and glaring eyes.

For he counteracts the Devil, who is death, by brisking about the life.

One feels how the cat touched the poet's heart:

For having considered God and himself, he will consider his neighbor.

For if he meets another cat he will kiss her in kindness.

For when he takes his prey he plays with it to give it a chance.

For one mouse in seven escapes by his dallying.

And one feels the poet's inspiration:

For he is of the Tribe of Tiger
For the Cherub Cat is a term of the Angel Tiger.

—Elizabeth Marshall Thomas

Christmas in New York

In the basement of my apartment building in New York City, I discovered a colony of wild cats. Moved by their plight, I began feeding them; but conditions down there became so bad that the cats were all infested with fleas and getting sick. One by one I trapped them, took them to the vet and had them cleaned up, inoculated, and neutered.

One of them, a female kitten I named Cleopatra, I brought home to my family, but she was so feral that I had to keep her locked in the bathroom so she wouldn't attack my other cats.

I tried to get close to her, to stroke her, and to show her that she wasn't in any danger, that she had found a home, and that she was loved. But she didn't trust anybody. Cleo wouldn't let me even touch her; she clawed me and bit me whenever I got too close. My hands and arms were covered in scratches and teeth marks.

Finally, when she had calmed down somewhat, I thought it was time to let Cleo have access to the rest of the apartment. The moment she was out of the bathroom she dashed under my bed and wouldn't leave, hiding there, refusing to come out even to eat. I wound up putting a food bowl and a litter pan under the bed, but that was an unsatisfactory arrangement.

What I really wanted was to have Cleo join the family and be my pet, but I saw that I'd have to start from scratch (and I mean scratch!). Figuring she'd have to go back to confinement in the bathroom for a while, I set up a small cat carrier there and pushed her food dish farther and farther back into it with each meal.

On Christmas Eve 1995, I decided to attend the Blessing of the Animals at Central Presbyterian Church—and to bring her along with me. Maybe in the presence of all those contented animals and devoted animal lovers Cleo would feel safe and begin to calm down and not be so frightened.

I have always believed there is something divine in the communion between people and animals—maybe this would bring it out in Cleo.

That evening, before going to the blessing, I sat and meditated, focusing entirely on the hope that Cleopatra would heal and be unafraid, that she would someday allow me to touch her.

With Cleo in the carrier, I took the subway from Brooklyn to Manhattan to the Central Presbyterian Church on Park Avenue and Sixty-fourth Street. On the train I took off my glove, baring my hand laced with scars and scratches, and tentatively opened Cleo's box. Slowly, I put my bare hand in and touched her very lightly on the back, and—

Nothing.

No hissing, no biting, none of her usual wild and frantic scratching.

No distrust at all. Just an amazing peace and quiet and the feel of her warm fur under my fingers.

My heart leaped as I realized that for the first time Cleopatra was allowing me to pet her. All during the train ride, I stroked her quietly. Once we were in the church, the woman sitting next to me put her hand into the carrier and stroked Cleo. Cleo accepted the stroking quietly and without resistance.

On the train ride home from the blessing it occurred to me I had a new cat. A shy, scared cat, but my cat.

That night, I was asleep in bed, when I woke up to a weight pressing against me. It was Cleo, curled up against my body and purring like a small engine as Christmas morning came. A great feeling of relief and gratitude washed over me as I received this little creature's love. From that night on, it was as though she'd always been with me, had never once been wild. All her fears were forgotten. Cleo was a sweet, gentle, loving pussycat. She was home.

To this day, I believe Cleo was a gift from God. My Christmas miracle.

—*Bill Edwards*

The Little Marine

Tory, my cat, was five years old when I found him at the Denver Dumb Friends League. Five years later, I had major surgery which kept me homebound for several months. A trip from the bedroom to the living room took a half hour—on a good day.

Overnight, Tory changed from a pet to a guardian with canine actions. He was by my side constantly—literally my shadow.

When I was in the living room, he was on the ottoman—eyes at half-mast, never ever closed.

When I was in the bedroom, he was at the foot of the bed, ever alert.

When I was in the shower, he was sitting beside the tub.

When I was in the kitchen, he was in the doorway.

The only time he truly slept was when my mother or friends he trusted were over to make meals and visit—or when I was asleep.

If I were in the living room or kitchen and he needed some solid sleep, he would curl around the legs of my walker, because he knew I couldn't go anywhere without using it—thus waking him.

If we were in the bedroom and someone came in the unlocked front door, he would bound off the bed and be in full attack mode—until he saw who the intruder was.

Overnight, he transformed himself from a happy-go-lucky critter into a guard cat who took his job very seriously.

We called him the little Marine.

Though still friendly, he would not leave my side to solicit attention from visitors—something he used to run to people for.

If they wanted to pet him, they had to come by me, and I had to give them permission to pet him.

He used to love to play; however, he knew that I simply couldn't, so he never solicited it.

That was almost two years ago. To this day, I marvel at the transformation this wonderful creature made to care for me in my months of need. When things seem difficult now, I think of how my little Marine summoned the strength to support me, and things seem easier. He is an inspiration to everyone who knows him.

Although I once thought this would be impossible, his devotion has deepened our bond immeasurably. I now love watching him curled up and sound asleep—not a care in the world—or bouncing over to company and throwing himself on their feet so they have to pet him.

I deny him almost nothing today. He gave up six months of his life to selflessly serve and protect me—the least I can do is play ball for half an hour in the evening, or join him on the balcony on balmy days—

and quietly watch this noble critter have a well-deserved rest.

—*Joan Drage*

Old Mother, Little Cat

On this particular December morning, I am having enough trouble as it is: troubles of the heart that can't be fixed as well as troubles that can be. Even as I kick an old towel around on the kitchen floor to sop up the leak from the dishwasher, I'm thinking of what I need to take to my mother today at the nursing home: mints, a small pillow for her paralyzed arm, the sharp scissors so I can give her a haircut—if the nurses have been able to convince her to sit up in the wheelchair for a while. I'm also making mental lists of the errands I have to run afterward.

So the floor won't flood, I grab the dripping towel and run with it to the back door. I do this automatically —I wring it out and hang it over the pool wall, I gather up the dry one from yesterday to lay it down under the leak. J., my good husband and man of the house, definitely plans to fix this leak; but I don't think he has the faintest idea of what is wrong. Still, he says he's not ready for me to call a plumber. He wants to think about it a little more.

My mind is everywhere at once; I need to do food shopping at the market after I see my mother. My college girls are coming home for the Christmas break in a few days, and I'll need lots more grains tables. (J. and I haven't quite given up our meat and buttered potatoes diet, though we've improved.)

I stand outside near the pool for a moment, watching the water drip from the towel, looking around at the bleak winter view, at the dead leaves on the deck, at the pecans from the tree floating like black beetles in the icy water.

A squadron of crows descends on the lawn, calling out with loud caws for others to join them to forage for newly fallen pecans. In this gray morning hour, the large birds, bent forward over their task, look like black stones on the paltry stretch of winter grass.

And it is then, just then, that I hear the cry. It seems to come almost from the tips of my toes—the saddest, most forlorn moan I have ever heard.

"What is it?" I cry automatically.

But there is only silence. Did I imagine it?

I look around now, alert and aware; I sense nothing but the faint movement of the trees in the chill winter wind (a cold wind, even for California) and the occasional clack of a crow.

I am about to go inside, when the sound comes again. It's an urgent sound, as close to a plea as it can be without words. Is it our old cat, Kitty, hurt or trapped? Even as I imagine this, Kitty appears on the pool wall, walking in his slow, majestic way, his great old gray coat thick and fluffed with winter fur. When the cry repeats itself we both hear it. Kitty freezes and stares at my feet. Nothing is there but patterns on the darkened concrete—the splotchy water stains that are dripping from the towel.

"What is it, where are you?" I say again. The cry is

vocal now, loud, full of pain, desperate. Then I see something just behind the wire screen that covers a square opening under the house, a crawl space to a place where no one ever goes. Something is pressed against the grids. I kneel down and see a pair of round green eyes looking back at me. They are both like little mouths open in terror.

"Oh my God," I say to Kitty. "It's some kind of creature."

The creature opens its mouth to cry out as if to verify this, and I hear the sound clearly and recognize it for what it is.

The meow of a kitten. Oh no. No, I won't think of it. Absolutely not. I won't consider it. I am done with these matters. I don't have the strength for it. I've done my duty: three children, a dog, dozens of mice, fish, birds, and two cats, one of which (Korky, the Beloved) we buried two years ago in the backyard at a solemn funeral rite.

Only old Kitty is left, and when he dies, which J. hopes will be in our lifetime, we can finally travel somewhere without endless arrangements and worries.

The hackles are up on Kitty's back; he wants no new friend, either. Fine. We're in agreement.

Go inside and forget about him. The next time you come out he'll be gone.

Even as I'm thinking this, I'm trying to pull the screen away from its frame, saying, "Shh, shh, don't be afraid, little one, you'll be fine, no one is going to hurt you." (Whose voice could this be? It can't be mine, not when I'm thinking something else entirely!) With a great heave of my arm (I wrench my back doing it), the rusted old screen comes away and the green eyes withdraw and vanish. I get a glimpse of something hopping, bunny-like, away into the dark recesses under the house.

My heart is full. I feel passionate, a long-gone sensation I barely recognize. I'm energized, full of purpose. I rush into the house and get a bowl and fill it with milk. I shake some of Kitty's dry food onto a plate. I don't say a word to J., who is reading the paper at the kitchen table. This will have to be a secret between me and Kitty, who has followed me into the house and whose eyes are narrowed as he watches me.

Outside again, I set the food dishes down in the place where I first saw the green eyes, in the hollow dark place under the house, on plain dirt. In the twenty-five years we've lived here, I've never really looked into this hole, into the cavernous darkness there. How could a kitten have gotten underneath, into this inhospitable cave? And why did he stay?

I wait, watching the food bowls, but there is no sound, no motion. Even Kitty, seeing that I have set out food, and having a passion for almost nothing else, does not try to venture there.

I look at him, fat and furred, in his thick gray coat. His enormous paws are like cartoon drawings. He, too, appeared in our lives as if by design on a day at least twelve years ago, now. J. was in the driveway with our daughters, all of them washing the station wagon. The kitten wandered shyly up to the bucket of suds and pitifully began to lap at the soapy water. J. shooed him away and a chorus of protests arose: "Ooooh, the poor thing." "Look how hungry he is!" "Oh, see how he's shivering."

"Don't anyone feed him," J. warned, "or he'll never leave."

Exactly! Our three daughters, as if by signal, dropped their rags, ran into the house and in half a minute brought out a feast: cream and raw eggs and bits of salami. The kitten ate ravenously, making gasping, almost sobbing sounds.

"He shouldn't eat so fast," said my youngest. "He might have to throw up." She then saw that the kitten had seven toes on one paw, and eight on the other "Oh no, he's a misfit," she cried. "We have to adopt him, so he'll feel loved."

"Don't even consider it," J. said. "And don't give him a name."

"We'll just call him Kitty," she told him, as if to reassure him that a generic title could prevent ownership. And so she did call him Kitty. And so did her sisters. And so did I. And so he has been called ever after.

Now I say to him, after all these many years that he has been called, merely, Kitty, "Don't worry, Big Kitty, we love you, too." And I realize that by naming him thus, I've just made room for one more.

—*Merrill Joan Gerber*

Velvet

I will never forget the first time I saw her. I was outside playing catch with my brother, and she just walked up to us and looked at us like we were supposed to keep her forever. How could we resist?

Velvet was the sweetest and most loving cat a little girl could ask for. I didn't have a lot of friends at that time in my life, but she was enough for me. Her fur always smelled like the fresh outside air, and I cried into it plenty of times. She was a really good listener; she never interrupted me when I told her what was going on in my life. If I was feeling sad she would just know, and she would come up to me and purr or meow until I stopped crying. She would stay in the bed with me if I was sick and wouldn't get up until I felt better. She didn't mind it when I put silly hats on her head or scarves around her neck and drank pretend tea with her. She didn't mind it when I called her "Velveeta" or "Sister Mary Velvet." Or that I picked her up all the time, even though I know she would rather have gone exploring on her own. She even came when I called her name, and she learned tricks.

I still see her soft blue eyes staring at me and I still feel her little paws digging into my stomach as she tries to make her bed. She slept on the other pillow of my double bed, and she didn't understand why this man was sleeping there in the few months before I had to put her to sleep. My biggest regret is that I let my fiancé convince me that she didn't have to sleep in the same room with us, and I shut the door to keep her out. I should have let her sleep with me like she always had for the last sixteen years, but I didn't. I know she was sleeping right outside the door wondering why I didn't let her in. I am so sorry, Velvet. You are so loved, yet I wonder if you thought I didn't love you near the end. Please forgive me.

She was so old and infirm. I don't think she could even see what was going on. She had to be lifted to her food dish and fed by hand, but I did that with love. I didn't mind feeding her that way. I didn't mind if she forgot where the litter box was. I wish I could have made her feel healthy again. But I had to end her suffering. I am glad I was there with her when the vet put her to sleep. I cried one more time into that soft fur until I could cry no more. I had to let go of her. But somewhere inside of me I never will be able to let go of my love for Velvet. I miss you every day, and I wish you were still here. I will never forget you, and I love you. I hope we will meet again someday. I still feel your presence when I am very sad. Please watch over me. I miss you so much, my friend and confidante.

—*Michele Perozzi*

A Cat Named Hope

When my teenage son had his first major disappointment in life, I was at a loss to help him. Rob was a senior in high school, and he felt his future closing in on him. He had spent months and all his money making a film to apply to film school—and the film had been ruined during sound editing. His girlfriend, his brother, and I tried to talk to him, but he just sat for what seemed like hours with his head in his hands. Our cat, Hope, curled at his feet.

My son's trials made me think about Hope, how she had had such a difficult start in life and had grown into the most affectionate animal in the house. She greets me at the door when I come home. She sleeps on my bed. She's at peace with everybody and helped bring a calm and peacefulness to our house, which isn't easy when you've got two teenage sons, a couple of cats and a dog!

To judge by our first meeting, I never would have guessed how much this cat would mean to our family. I'd seen her and her four kittens one day when I was volunteering at the local animal shelter. When I opened the cage to hold her, a staff member shouted a warning, "That cat is a terror!" But I saw that the mother cat was just scared in the crowded and noisy shelter and was determined to protect her babies.

Time was running out quickly on the mother and her kittens at the animal shelter. At the end of the day, I took the little family home, hoping I could foster them for a while and find them all homes later.

The mother cat was nervous and hostile in our house. When the kittens were ready, I brought the family back to the shelter for adoption. The kittens soon found good homes, but their mother wasn't so lucky—after a few days at the shelter, she got sick. I didn't know what it was about this cat, but I missed her. I took her home again from the shelter, figuring I'd nurse her back to health and put her back up for adoption. I still didn't even know her name.

But back at the shelter a third time, the mother cat, now healthy and adoptable, went ballistic! I had to get her out again! This time, I rushed to the veterinarian to have this "terror" spayed; I thought it would calm her down and make her more adoptable. I was so frustrated when I got her to the vet's that when the receptionist asked for the cat's name I blurted out, "I don't know! She's hopeless!"

Later, in the parking lot, it suddenly dawned on me. The cat had escaped the animal shelter not once, but *three* times. She'd beaten incredible odds and never gave up. Her name was obvious!

That afternoon we didn't even notice her near my son's feet. I held my breath as I watched Rob try to cope with his disappointment. At last, he stood up and stumbled, almost stepping on the cat. With a grin on his face he looked at us and said, "I almost stamped out Hope." The phrase became an inspiration in our household. Years later, we still use it on those days when we need encouragement. My son married his girlfriend, went on to film school and became a successful television producer, and our wonderful cat is still with us. All of which proves you can't stamp out Hope in this household.

—Dee Sheppe

CHAPTER FOUR

Loyalty and Friendship

A dog, quick as a rowboat to your side, is your best friend in a minute. A cat, turning slowly like the great ocean liner, is your friend for life.

Anonymous

Our philosophy is "A home without a cat is just a house."

Shirle Collings

The Old Cat Poem

The letter from the old woman in California, with a cat poem she had read sixty years ago in the *Chicago Tribune* and never forgotten, made me realize that people have not changed. Nor have their cats and dogs. Not in sixty years or six thousand years. I was sitting at my computer on Shady Oak Farm, rushing to meet a deadline, when I opened the small, typewritten letter, and the small cat poem fell out; and I raised my eyes for the first time that morning to watch our dogs gamboling over our land. I noticed the stand of pines beyond the fence line and the sun lying golden on the fields.

I felt for the first time that morning the small wet patch on my wrist where my border collie mix, who has shadowed me every living minute since I adopted him, who sleeps in my bedroom and watches me take a shower, had been nudging me to get my attention. My faithful rough-coated black-white-copper-silver-gray friend with the ferociously wagging tail and the Frisbee in his mouth.

The small cat poem, written anonymously in the 1930s, passed on to me by Ann Wugan in California from memory after all these years, had made me stop and absorb the wonder of the moment, had given me a warm feeling inside.

It is fashionable to hear in the media today that, with all the world's problems, people have changed. Human beings today are different than they were in our grandparent's time, in that simpler, more virtuous age. Folks were stronger then, more self-reliant, more devoted to their families and neighbors. This news comes to us from what the ancient Romans called the *negotium*— the public world, with its politics and cities. The ancient Romans, senators and poets alike, are on record as being desperately eager to flee the *negotium* and return to the *otium*—their country villas, where they lingered in harmony with the deeper truths of friends, food, animals. People have not changed in the smallest bit.

It is true, however, that our pets show us how far we have drifted from a more natural way of life, from the days of wholeness in that Eden that once existed in the soul of all peoples, of all faiths, from the days of harmony with living things.

"No one can give anyone else the gift of the idyll," the great novelist Milan Kundera writes in *The Unbearable Lightness of Being*. "Only an animal can do so, because only animals were not expelled from Paradise."

What does this mean? It means cats and dogs point the way back to the idyll, remind us how to experience what the French philosopher Mircea Eliade called "sacred time"—the timeless feeling that comes with living by the seasons, by the sun, by stroking your cat as he stretches by the fire. The wonderful, deeply human-canine-feline feeling of living outside "the horror of time," the myth of history humans have invented.

It's fashionable, too, to hear in our modern age that the difference between people and animals is the human knowledge of death, our awareness of time. But this, too, is false. Elephants who weep over the death of their kin are briefly, painfully aware of time; the man who works at his computer all day pressing to meet a deadline until his dog nudges, licks, noses his wrist with wet pleas until finally the man rises, "Yes, I'll play Frisbee with you, if you'll just leave me alone!"—that man, whose heart soars as he throws a Frisbee for his dog on a summer day, is blissfully, briefly free of time.

We have not changed. Our animals have not changed. We have drifted away. And our cats and dogs call us back.

In my wedding vow, after slipping on her finger the gold band carved with the likeness of our home, my ancestor's sailing ship, palm trees, the rising sun, grapevines, a cabbage, and our dog, I told my wife, "Your love is in my heart like the reed in the arms of the wind." This was written by an Egyptian, a cat lover, no doubt, five thousand years ago, decoded from hieroglyphics early in this century by a man who felt it just as the writer intended and passed it on to me.

These things came to my mind when the small cat poem fell out of the small envelope from the woman in California.

"Long ago, about 1938, I think," Ann wrote, "I saw the following verse in the 'Line of Type or Two' in the *Chicago Tribune*. I do not remember the name of the author."

Ann's letter was dated 1996. She remembered everything else about the small poem about cats she had read in the newspaper one morning in Chicago almost sixty years earlier.

MY CAT
Close by a wall
Whose bricks were all
Rainsoaked and old
A little cat
Hunched where he sat
Shivering and cold.

Deaf to his cry
Crowds hurried by
Past his meow.
I couldn't bear
To see him there.
He's my cat now.

We have long talks
Lincoln Park walks
Cream puffs and pie
A window pane
Shuts out the rain
Keeps my cat dry.

— *Anonymous*

   After I read the poem, I thought of Blaga Dimitrova, who said, "A cat stretches from one end of my childhood to the other."

   And I went out and threw the Frisbee to my dog until my heart, too, began to soar on invisible currents under the hawks and clouds. And the swift, strong mutt ran them down like a receiver for the gods, until he told me it was time to stop. And lying on the dirt, through heaving contented breaths, he smiled at me.

   And I thought about what Ann had taught me:

   A cat stretches from one end of life to the other.

   A cat stretches from one century to the other.

   A cat stretches by the fire.

— *Michael Capuzzo*

Christmas in Miami

John Patrick O'Neill could live with his secret no longer. Alone and jobless, O'Neill, fifty, shared his home with four stray cats, his only friends. They all lived together under the east bridge of the MacArthur Causeway. From the gloom under the bridge, as traffic rumbled by overhead, they could see the city skyline, the holiday lights, and the million-dollar Star Island homes of the rich and famous. On Christmas Eve, the animals lost their friend and protector.

At dark, as motorists whizzed past, O'Neill trudged more than a mile to Miami Beach police headquarters. It was Christmas Eve, and he wanted to confess. He had killed a man, he said, and buried the corpse beneath the bridge where he lived.

O'Neill had a reason. The man he killed, who was also homeless, had hurled his beloved cats, all four of them, into Biscayne Bay to drown. The thrashing, panicky animals were unable to climb the sheer concrete embankment, but O'Neill had jumped into the water after them. He rescued them, then turned to confront the man who tried to drown them.

The man, Daniel Francis Kelly, fifty-eight, pulled a knife and lunged at him, O'Neill said. O'Neill punched and stomped Kelly until he was dead, then dug a shallow grave with his hands and a piece of board.

That was on Friday, December 19. Now, on Christmas Eve, he wanted to clear his conscience.

Police were doubtful, but detectives Nick Lluy and Robert Hanlon listened. "He wasn't drunk," Hanlon said later. "It sounded plausible."

Everybody hoped it was not true. Everybody wanted to go home. The detectives went out to the east bridge and descended into the darkness. They scanned with flashlights, probed the ground under the bridge, and found a suspicious mound, emitting an even more suspicious odor.

A fire truck with high-intensity lights arrived to illuminate the area, directly across from the Miami Beach Coast Guard base. The detectives sent for shovels and generators and began to dig.

About to leave the *Herald* for Christmas Eve services, I heard something was afoot and called police headquarters. Detective Anthony Sabatino had just bought O'Neill a double hamburger, microwaved at a 7-Eleven. "This is a heckuva way to spend Christmas," the detective said.

He was right.

I went out to the scene to see what they would find. The underside of the bridge is a haven to street people. A number of urban Bedouins had camped there from time to time. There were couches and chaise longues, even a little Christmas tree with tinsel.

Police spokesman Howard Zeifman cautioned that it might be a hoax. "People have lived under here for years," he said. "It smells of rotten food, human waste, and cats."

It did.

But the story was no hoax. Cops, a prosecutor, a medical examiner, and firefighters labored through the night, watched by a cautious full-grown calico and a curious, half-grown black cat with a white bib. By Christmas morning the shallow grave had yielded the remains of a dead man, and O'Neill was charged with second-degree murder.

"I feel kind of sad for the guy," said Hanlon, a veteran detective. "If he didn't come in and tell us about it, there's a very good chance that we never would have found it. I guess it was bothering him."

Identified through fingerprints, the dead man had an arrest record nineteen pages long, mostly for drunkenness, vagrancy, and disorderly conduct. He was remembered by police as a "nasty drunk." Hanlon himself had arrested Kelly once. A Christmas Day autopsy confirmed that death was caused by blows to the head.

In his jail cell, O'Neill worried about his friends. He called the calico the Bandit. The black with the bib was Smokey. Satchmo was a striped gray, and the Tiger was white with golden stripes. O'Neill was served a Christmas Day dinner of roast beef, but nobody fed them.

"I'm just sorry about my cats," he told Hanlon. The detective tried to catch them, to take them to the humane society, but they scampered away; and he had no time to spend in their pursuit.

My story appeared, and *Herald* readers who care about animals created a minor traffic jam on the causeway. One woman rescued three of the cats and took them home. She never found Satchmo. "They were well, well taken care of," she said. "These were not stray cats."

John O'Neill pleaded not guilty, and I talked to him after his arraignment. He said he was not a killer. "It was self-defense. I had five lives to protect. Four of them were my cats." The fifth, he said, was his own.

He said the cats were better friends than some people. He had found each of them on Miami Beach, lost, abandoned, and hungry. He had rescued them, one by one, and taken them home, to his place under the bridge. It was home to him.

"I sure love the water," he said. "I feel free there. I like it, it's outside, no rent, no nothing. I always had cat food for them. I fed them seven o'clock in the morning. When I left in the morning, I always left a big bowl of water. I also had vitamins for them. When I came home at five or six o'clock, I would feed them again and give them fresh water."

His days were busy in Miami Beach, "picking up and recycling aluminum cans, so I could feed them and myself. I also got my beer and my smokes out of it. That was my daily routine, going to get cans and feeding my cats."

Kelly disrupted the routine the week before Christmas. Other homeless men often shared the space under the bridge, and he was one of them. He snatched up O'Neill's friends—the Bandit, the Tiger, Smokey, and Satchmo—and threw them into the bay.

"They were clinging to the seawall," O'Neill said. He saved them, then faced their attacker. "If you ever do that again, I'll break your jaw!" Kelly pulled a butcher knife, he said, and rushed him. O'Neill punched, kicked, and stomped the man.

"What I did was for them. I just went on hitting him." This was the first time such a thing had ever happened to him. He did like to drink and admitted his share of trouble, "but never violence."

He had lived with the burden of his secret five days and nights, then couldn't stand the guilt anymore. A practicing Catholic, he said, "I had to get it off my chest." Jailed without bond, he would stand trial in the spring.

I asked if he wanted me to contact anyone. His mother still lived in Port Chester, New York, where he grew up along the coast of Long Island Sound, fourteen hundred miles north of Miami. She was unaware of his trouble.

"I haven't written her," he told me. "If it was something else, it would be easy, but I don't know how to tell her this."

At the office I heard from a shocked reader, a man who had grown up with O'Neill in Port Chester, where he was known as Teedy O'Neill.

"He was a leader, the one you always chose first for a

baseball team," said the boyhood friend. "He was a tough, athletic kid but never a bully." Teedy O'Neill was a drifter and a loner even then, "an outdoorsy-type guy who would just drift in and out of school. He was a hero, a good guy. He wouldn't hurt anybody. He wouldn't pick on anybody. Is he a bum? No, he is not a bum. It takes quite a man to confess when his conscience bothers him."

Stories went out on the newswire, and letters of support came from animal lovers all over the country.

A jury deliberated for an hour that spring before returning a not guilty verdict. They believed it was self-defense. The woman who cared for Smokey, the Bandit, and the Tiger found O'Neill a place to stay and work at an auto dealership.

The temperature was eighty. It was April in Miami. But it finally felt like Christmas.

—*Edna Buchanan*

The Arrival

Back then, there were Chevrolet families and Buick families. *Life* magazine families and *Look* magazine families. Dog families and cat families.

We were a dog family, the Davises. We were disdainful of cats. But cats have a way of entering the hardest hearts and staying there.

It was 1947—that golden time when John Cheever said New York City was suffused with a river light and gentlemen wore hats—and we lived in a New Jersey suburb. Every day my father took the bus to New York City to work.

The blizzard that hit New York and New Jersey in 1947 brought the first cat ever to enter the Davis home. In the early stages of the storm, a small, young pregnant cat appeared on our doorstep. Knowing the cat would freeze to death if left out, my dad reluctantly allowed her inside, with the proviso that she *must* leave when the storm passed.

You know the next part. The cat knew just whose heart she had to capture (my dad's) and set about doing it. By the time the storm was over (four days later), "Kit" and my dad were inseparable. And Kit quickly went about converting all us Davises to a cat family, too. Whenever my mom and dad went to see neighbors, Kit walked along, perched on an outside windowsill of the neighbor's house, waited for my parents to enjoy their little visit, then accompanied them home.

But it was my dad whom Kit loved best.

Early each morning, my dad walked two blocks to the corner to get the bus to New York City to go to work. By spring, Kit was joining my dad on his walk to the bus each day. She'd see him off and then return home to wait for her best pal.

Dad came home on the 6:00 bus each evening. At

precisely 5:50, Kit would come downstairs, meow at the door to be let out, and walk to the corner to wait for the bus. She and my dad would walk home together.

One day, eleven years later, Kit's world changed. A heart attack took my dad, and the light went out of Kit's life. She stopped eating and began to mope around the house, clearly depressed, refusing all attention. No amount of petting or play would cheer her.

Two months later, she joined my dad.

Thanks to that little refugee from a storm, I have owned and loved cats ever since. But I have never even heard of one who did what that lost stray, Kit, did. Whenever I think of her I remember the winter of 1947, my dad, and the dog family that became a cat family forever.

—*Marilyn Barry*

Whisper to Me

We got our cat Whisper at a local SPCA. She was beautiful and had a personality like none other. She went with us everywhere. We have a travel trailer, and Whisper spent a few months in it with us each year, seeing the world. Other than that, Whisper was a stay-at-home cat.

Our bedroom window faced a small patch of grass. On the other side was a home with a bedroom window just like ours. There a frail, tiny widow would sit and watch. Whisper sat at her window and watched too. Nature provided all the entertainment they needed. When spring came, the woman would open the window just a bit and call softly to the cat. Sometimes the cat would respond to the woman, rubbing her head against the screen. And so the ritual went on, day and night. Our little cat was living up to her name—she and Ruth whispered away the hours to each other.

They both liked to stay inside. The outside was often frightening but not from the windows. In the evening there were shadows and cars to see. But that winter, Ruth became very ill. When she came to the window, it seemed that Whisper spent more time in her window across the patch of grass, checking on her friend. When the woman felt well enough they would watch rabbits scampering and playing in the snow.

One cold day the woman was gone. Her tiny body could no longer fight her illness. When Whisper went to the window, her partner wasn't there. My husband called the florist.

Later, the florist called us back, a little confused. "Is this the right name? Whiskers? Or is it Whisper? I don't think we ever did this before."

Maybe it was a stupid idea. Flowers at a funeral . . . from a cat. We worried that it was inappropriate. We stood at the cemetery during the funeral thinking about spring and the birds and forsythia and Ruth's brown sparkling eyes that would no longer see any of it.

Lost in thought we didn't notice the young woman who touched my husband's arm. "I'm so glad you put her name on the card. Mom talked about her a lot. She was a great pastime for her. Thank you."

As my husband and I walked back to the car, we felt everything was okay. It was only right that our cat told her dear window friend good-bye.

Sometimes, when one tree dies, another, just a few feet away, will follow. So it was that Whisper became gravely ill and died of a rare kidney disease that brought on numerous complications. Too many, even, for our weeks of medicine, hospital visits, and love.

We spent the last night together in our bed. My husband held Whisper in his arms all night. Every five or ten minutes he would hold her up as she cried and gasped for breath. Then she would settle into his arms again.

In the morning we knew there was only one thing to do. It was the most difficult thing we had ever done but we held her and petted her speaking gently all the while as the sedative took its toll and she fell asleep forever. There was no struggle. She went peacefully. We cried buckets of tears but she was still gone.

We know better, but we still look for her to greet us at the door when we come home. Still wait for her to jump onto the bed as soon as we turn in for the night. Our little furry friend loved us unconditionally and even had some left over for the old woman next door. She only hoped that we would love her back, and we did it with all our hearts. We have our memories, and they will never die. She is Whisper to me forever.

—*Miriam A. Roland*

The Cat Who Was
Always There

Studzey was the stray who was always there, haunting our yard. Again and again he appeared out of the blue for a visit—but just to eat and run, never staying long. We never knew where he came from or where he was going. But one night, during a storm, Studzey came to us with a look in his eyes and a tilt to his head that seemed to say, "It's time." My daughter saw his soaking fur coat and muddy paws and took pity. Studzey accepted her invitation inside and made himself quite comfortable that night and the night after that. Maybe because he was a stray he had the gift of never letting anything get in the way of what he needed—and it was a home he needed now.

After a few days, we realized happily that Studzey was ours for good. We had to officially adopt him and make a trip to the vet for neutering and a health check. It was then we learned that our Studzey had an advanced case of feline leukemia. The vet recommended we put him to sleep rather than go through an awful ordeal. Studzey had six months to live, perhaps less, the vet said. We were devastated. We had fallen in love with him, and he was already very much a part of our family.

I looked at Studzey. In his eyes I saw contentment, gentleness, a sense of belonging. Studzey was three years old and probably a stray most of his life, the vet said. I thought, how unfair for such a loving cat to have never known the warmth of a family. That made the decision. The least we could do was give him a wonderful home for the last months of his life.

The vet recommended that he not be an outside cat anymore due to his illness. That was fine with us—and fine with Studzey. Our roaming tom suddenly had no desire to run out of the house even when a door was open. It was as though he had had enough of the cruel world out there and preferred the warmth of a home.

Whenever I looked up, Studzey was lounging on a sofa or bed. Seeking comfort, curling up against us wherever we were, purring away—these were his chief pleasures. He became our cat who was always there.

To our astonishment, Studzey breezed through the first six months. And the second six months. And six months after that. After three years of remarkable health, considering his disease, the vet was amazed. His only explanation was that Studzey was so happy and loved he managed to fight off the worst of his disease.

Every morning I would find him lying across my chest—almost as if he couldn't get close enough to me. When I would walk into the room, he would look up, and I would see what looked like a smile on his face with his eyes blinking constantly. If we watched TV, he'd jump on our laps and push his nose in our face telling us that he wanted his head scratched. If you stopped scratching, he'd smack your chin with his paw to remind you to continue, please. Studzey always let us know he was there.

When I got ready for work, he'd bat my legs with his paws when I got out of the shower until I fed him. When we got home at the end of the day, Studzey would greet us—then follow us all over the house me-owing loudly until we fed him; perhaps because we fed him salmon. And when he couldn't digest dry cat food, we discovered Studzey had a taste for chocolate chip ice cream. Studzey and I shared many a night watching a movie and enjoying our chocolate chip ice cream to-gether. He was my baby, and I was so close to him.

When I brought home my future husband, there was Studzey giving him the once-over that first date and every date after that. My husband eventually got Studzey's final approval, and they became close friends.

Then one weekend, after three years, Studzey was so weak he could hardly move. The medication that had helped him with his various ailments didn't seem to be working anymore. He curled up on his favorite spot on the sofa and slept through the day, refusing to eat, even when I warmed his food to soothe his swallowing. When I petted him, he lifted his head and smiled, but I knew he didn't have much time. That night, I stayed with him for hours and said good-bye through my tears. I knew the next morning I had to bring Studzey to the vet.

When I woke up the next morning, my husband told me that Studzey had peacefully passed away. God had made the decision for me. I was very upset, but then my husband told me the rest of his story.

He had gotten up that Sunday morning early, careful not to wake me because of the rough night I had with Studzey. He went outside to get the paper, stopping to check on Studzey, who'd spent the night on the sofa, being too weak to climb upstairs. When he patted our kitty's head, Studzey lifted his head and purred. My husband talked to Studzey and patted him for a while before returning upstairs to me, quietly closing the door to read the paper.

A short time passed and my husband looked up from the paper and saw Studzey sitting there in front of him. He looked down at the paper but then suddenly realized that he had closed the door, how could Studzey have come into the room? When he looked again, Studzey was no longer there. He got up and looked at the door and it was still closed. Puzzled, he then went downstairs to check on Studzey, and it was then he found Studzey had passed away, lying so still on the sofa still warm. To this day, my husband believes that

Studzey had come upstairs to say good-bye to him. After all, I had already said my good-byes to him the night before, but my husband hadn't. We miss Studzey very much. We are so grateful to have stolen four wonderful years with our cat who was always there.

—Helena Marchant

My Cat Clyde

There must be many wonderful stories about remarkable cats and their equally remarkable lives, but the cat I want to tell you about did none of these things: He was never lost and never found his way home from hundreds of miles away. He never saved a life. He never learned to do tricks or impress my friends with his extraordinary intelligence.

Cats are not generally known for the quality of their devotion. They are frequently derided for being cold and distant animals, primarily interested in satisfying their need for food and shelter, with the human element being a tolerated convenience. It was a great gift, therefore, to be loved unshakably and unwaveringly by an animal with this reputation. If my cat was remarkable in any way, beyond the way all cats are remarkable, it was in the way in which he was able to love. His devotion to me, and only me, would have put the greatest dog to shame.

In 1981 I found myself at the local humane society staring at dozens of kittens up for adoption. I was leaning against one of the cages and narrowing my choice down to one in a litter of tabbies, when I felt two small, soft paws wrap themselves around my arm. I turned and looked into a pair of bright, lima green eyes. Holding tighter, a tiny white kitten with orange tabby markings stared at me with determination, then threw his head back and yowled. Loudly. Very loudly. There to choose, I had been undeniably chosen. Without hesitation, I turned to the woman helping me and said, "I'll take this one." Two weeks later, having met the necessary criteria, I brought my little bundle of joy home.

Within moments of our arrival, a loud noise frightened my kitten and he shot under the sofa. He was up against the back wall, terrified. I pressed myself to the floor and softly tried to coax him out. He blinked. In that moment he made a decision from which he would never back down and crawled straight out into my arms.

Clyde grew into one of the largest cats I have ever seen. He meowed constantly from the moment I brought him home. He stopped only to sleep and purr. He would remain stoically (and amazingly!) silent during overnight visits to the vet, but would inevitably break into loud calls at the sound of my voice. He was my companion during many dark, lonely years; and I cared for him devotedly through numerous, frightening illnesses. When leaving the house, I could hear him meowing through the door as I walked away. On my return, he was always there to greet me. When he was frightened, he would bury his face in my chest; and when he was happy, he would blink at me and smile broadly. During affectionate moments, he would mimic my meow to him in quiet conversation. He would turn up his nose in disdain at a can of tuna, but loved spaghetti sauce and would become ecstatic if I gave him an olive.

I could tell you endless stories of his misadventures, but none would vary much from the misadventures of other cats. He was handsome, he was funny, he was an unbelievable pain; but mostly, Clyde was just completely mine . . . and I was completely his.

I suppose that fourteen years pass quickly for everyone. The day finally came when, his liver failing from a long fight with diabetes, I made the decision to end Clyde's suffering. Because he could no longer jump onto the bed, I spent his last night with him on the floor. He curled up in the crook of my arm and I think he purred all night.

Knowing that he would die terrified if I brought him to his vet's office, I requested a final home visit. It was the last gift I could give him. So, it was on a warm June morning that I held my dear cat close as he yelled his protest and the vet administered one final shot. Three last meows and the ever-present voice of my constant companion was silenced forever. I wonder if I will ever mourn another friend in the same way.

I know that never again in my life am I likely to find the kind of devotion and complete, remarkable love I had from this one cat. Someday I will have to face what lies beyond; but it seems a little easier knowing that first in line, hurrying to meet me and yelling his head off, will be my cat Clyde.

—*Katherine Egbert O'Rourke*

The Cat Who Came to Stay

There's a cat story that has been in our family for a long time. It's one my mother told us and that happened when she was a girl living in a basement apartment in Greenwich Village in New York City. This happened in 1902, by the way. Basement apartments have windows at street level. The cat was a large black-and-white tiger who appeared at the street-level window one day, meowing and tapping the glass. For days this cat tried hard to adopt my mother's family but my grandmother was strongly against it. No cats!

One morning the family arose, and there on the kitchen floor in a circle (a "perfect circle," my mother used to say) were nine big rats (dead) and the cat in the middle, complacently washing her face. She knew that to be assured of her chosen home she had to be a contributing member. This was back when folks had to earn their keep, my mother used to say, and so did cats. Grandma never issued a peep of protest about the new family member after that.

—Ann Di Lorenzo

Mr. Mac

Mr. Mac was a friend who shared my way of life for fourteen years. I could do no wrong in his eyes, or he in mine. He was a black-and-white American Shorthair with a kindly disposition who even tolerated tail-grabbing grandchildren. We adapted to each other's ways—he slept when I slept; he ate when I ate. When I gardened he watched, when I put feed in the feeders, he watched. Even when a family of quail marched follow-the-leader across the patio—he watched. He never climbed a tree or scared away a ground-feeding bird. He was a thoroughly nice cat.

Our mornings had a wonderful routine. We'd rise very early, around four, and sit in the living room with the windows open enjoying the warm Florida breeze. I'd read while he purred in my lap. When we heard the thump of the newspaper's delivery, we'd walk out to get it, me, like Mr. Mac, barefoot. No need for the porch light. I could see the paper by the light of the street lamp.

One morning, we heard the paper arrive, left our chair, and went to the front door. Suddenly, as my hand touched the doorknob, Mr. Mac drew back and meowed loudly.

I was astonished and thought that perhaps a stray cat had invaded his territory. I snapped on the porch light as I opened the door; and there, on the doorstep, where my bare foot would have landed, was a poisonous coral snake! Mr. Mac ran out while I went back for shoes and a shovel. I found my hero cat trailing the snake down the street. I quickly used the shovel to dispatch the snake. Mr. Mac got a kiss and a tight squeeze, and my everlasting gratitude.

—*Christine Edward*

A Life with Sam

At the age of four, I named our family cat "Sam" because he was a "samanese" cat. His first day home, he hid his scrawny, peach fuzz–covered body under a cart until we were able to coax him out with food. "Why won't he come out?" I remember asking my mom over the din of five other squawking children. "He needs to get used to his new home," my mom assured me.

By the time I had turned five, Sam had become very handsome and majestic looking, and he was my favorite playmate. I would start on the third floor of our house; and with Sam at my heel, I tore down two flights of stairs, through the den, then the dining room, only to stop at the entrance to the kitchen. Sam never stopped, though, hitting the slippery, claw-impervious flooring as if he were on ice, skidding into the refrigerator door eight feet away like a cartoon cat. While I giggled, Sam would walk off poised as if he had meant to do that.

At the age of seven, I had the warmest sleeping partner in the world in Sam, whose white, gray, and black furred, muscular body would fit neatly in the crook of my bended knees as I lay on my side, listening to him purr.

When, at the age of eight, my family went on a month's vacation, we left Sam in the care of friends. "He'll be fine," my mom reassured herself as much as us. Upon returning, Sam had chewed away the fur halfway up his long, sleek, dark tail and gave us unforgiving looks. I wouldn't doubt that this was calculated on his part as we treated him like a king for days, and we never left him for that amount of time again.

Sam matured as I matured; and as I saw more of friends and school and the world outside, he saw less of me. But we were still partners. There was always a place for him on my lap, and he always had time for me to brush him. We got into trouble together, too. I'm sure it was Sam's idea when I accidentally lit the curtains on fire, but he always seemed to escape my mother's wrath. Even when Sam was unable to reach his litterbox one time and did his business in a shoe, my mom wasn't angry but commented on how neat Sam had been containing it in a shoe. He was a friend to all guests at our house, managing somehow to choose the only lap in a group whose owner didn't like cats. We'd offer to take him away, but such guests wouldn't have him removed, possibly sensing that he was part of the family.

Sam helped me with my homework while at the same time managing to take a number of naps underneath the warm lamp on the desk. He also helped my dad with his checkbook, my mom with her letters, my brothers with their term papers; and as a matter of fact, he helped with anything that was going on at the desk at night when the lamp was on.

When I was fifteen, Sam developed cataracts. When I was sixteen, he went blind in one eye and suffered poor vision in the other. When I was seventeen, Sam was having problems making his way through the house without bumping into things, like the refrigerator he'd slid into playfully as a kitten. With tears in our eyes, my mom and I made the difficult decision to take him to his last visit to the vet. I couldn't bear to go. My mom held him when they gave him his injection. She said he didn't struggle much, that he was a good cat until the end.

Since then, our family has cared for many more cats, but mom and I still tell stories about Sam. I get teary-eyed thinking about him and cried as I wrote this, fourteen years after his death.

I'm thirty-one years old now, and I will always have Sam.

—*Margot Callahan*

Mauzer and Me

Nearly twenty years ago, on a stormy Memorial Day, I was driving down a rain-filled highway, when I saw a small gray ball in the middle of the road. As I drove by, it moved. When I stopped to retrieve it, it fit in the palm of my hand, a small gray kitten. I bathed him in a warm tub of water; and for the next twenty years, he enjoyed having his face gently washed with warm water. His head was swollen, and the vet did surgery not expecting the cat to live, but Mauzer sure fooled him.

Our life for seventeen years was much as any other cat and owner, full of love, jealousy, arrogance, teasing, and playing, with him always the boss! In that seventeenth year, I became ill and almost immobile with severe rheumatoid arthritis. I was in much pain, and many surgeries to the joints did little to relieve it. Mauzer became my surrogate nurse, companion—whatever I needed. He wouldn't leave my side. If I became depressed he would put his foot on my nose to entice me to play an old game we played. If that didn't work, he would push as close as he could to my body and talk and purr as loud as he could as if to say: "I'm here, I care."

I was alone and in pain, and some mornings I would not have gotten up except for his coaxing me to get up by purring and rubbing my hands, ever patient waiting to be fed. The trip from the bedroom to the kitchen with my walker sometimes took five or ten minutes, not to mention the time opening the can; then resting to make the trip back to bed with the coffee, I always had Mauzer either in front of the walker or behind it (or often keeping my attention focused by weaving and rubbing inside the legs of the walker). For two lonely, difficult years I don't know if I would have ever left my bed if my friend didn't need to go out, come in or be fed; but never did he push me to do these things, caring for me first, purring and talking to me while I rested. Slowly I became stronger with the love of my Mauzer to support me, ever patient.

I'm up and around now, and Mauzer spends more time outside because he knows I don't need him so much to cheer me and get me through the day. My wonderful old friend is twenty years old now; and I noticed he has lost some teeth and is gumming it, so I cut his food smaller. Sometimes he doesn't want to jump off the bed to go out, so I carry him to the door. Other times he can't jump on the porch table to be brushed, so I lift him up and comb and brush him. Mauzer doesn't have as much energy anymore to play games. But at night before we go to sleep, he puts his paw on my nose, and I brush my fingers across his nose and eyes a few times. Then he pushes up close and talks and purrs all night: "I'm here, I care!"

—*Irene Juanico*

CHAPTER FIVE

Cat Nipped My Funny Bone

Your cat will never threaten your popularity by barking at three in the morning. He won't attack the mailman or eat the drapes, although he may climb the drapes to see how the room looks from the ceiling.

Helen Powers

Dogs come when they're called; cats take a message and get back to you.

Mary Bly

The Day The Luke Flew

My husband and I own an inn in Cape May, New Jersey, with nine rooms and forty-two cats. This is more cats than sane people like to admit to owning, but we are sane and all our cats well cared for. Having so many cats as well as human companions has given us a world of richness.

At the bottom of our inn stationery is a quote from Anaïs Nin:

Each friend represents a world in us,
A world possibly not born until they arrive,
And it is only by this meeting that a new world is
  born

A small new world of glee opens up for anyone who meets The Luke, our three-year-old ginger tabby.

The Luke has a long list of most unusual habits. He leaves each morning at daybreak for a two-hour morning swim at the nearby marsh. He returns at approximately 7:30, barrels through the cat door, dripping from the tips of his ears to the end of his tail, and loudly announces that he is now ready for breakfast. During August, The Luke takes two swims a day even though the marsh is considerably down. He returns wet, but his feet and legs are that lovely algae green.

The Luke is a perfectly striped marmalade tabby with white feet and a white blaze. He greets me each day with a loud "Ye-*ow*" and then stands upright on his back feet and does a two-step, which I call the poodle pirouette.

The Luke had a bad winter last year. His refusal to let me tend his sore gums had resulted in a dramatic weight loss from twelve to a mere eight pounds. His stripes stood out like grotesque skeleton bones, and the poodle pirouette had been reduced to a half buck and a sad little mee-eu. We did our best to make him comfortable; but the vet said The Luke had to let us medicate him for him to get better.

Things didn't improve until one sunny day in spring. That was the day The Luke decided to fly. Billy, our thirteen-year-old dominant male cat, once flew on a dog's back. He leaped up on the neck of a Labrador and rode him to the end of the block until the dog and owner cowered in retreat. But this was the day The Luke outdid even the top cat.

We had all assembled in the garden to work. Well, we raked and the cats watched. The Luke had taken up a quiet spot under the picnic table, where he watched the sharp teeth of the rake go back and forth digging up fresh moist earth.

The heavens began to fill with the screaming sounds of seagulls, and my cats began leaving the garden as the gulls landed on the mounds of dirt. I set my rake aside to shoo them away. Then The Luke like an emaciated fireball shot out from under the picnic table and tore past me. I watched in horror as he leaped with one bound and landed spread-eagle on the back of a young gull. His paws clung to the front wings, his back feet curled about the tail. In that moment, the gull's wing span unfurled to what seemed like eight feet, and the feathered beast lifted off the ground with my baby Luke hanging on for dear life.

I began bellowing like a gut-shot wildebeest. "No! No!" I screeched but to no avail. The gull climbed two feet and continued flying—my Luke attached. Images of a Lukey-lunch being served in tiny pucks to gobbling seagulls flashed through my mind. My panic rose; and I stumbled, spraining my ankle and tumbling to the ground.

At that instant, my husband bounded onto the scene, no doubt with butterflies in his stomach over what heroics I was going to ask him to perform now. Once I trapped a wild kitten in the bathroom and told him to go in there and put her in the kennel. Half an hour later, he emerged with his hair tussled, shirt torn, bleeding from a scratch and bite on his arm, and announced, "Don't ever tell me to do that again!" But this time he didn't have to do anything but watch as the thieving seagull flipped sideways and rolled The Luke off into the mint garden. A tiny, orange head popped up with a large tail feather held between its red lips. The gull flew away as did the rest of the flock. The Luke carried the tail feather around all day for all the cats to see.

The day The Luke flew was the prelude to an excellent summer for him. He went swimming each and every day. His front little beaver teeth fell out soon after the gull-riding incident, and his gums have healed nicely. His weight has increased to a healthy, toned fourteen pounds.

As we sit together writing this, The Luke and I realize that spring can't be far away. We can hardly wait for the day those thieving gulls return. The Luke smiles a charming toothless grin—I know what he has on his mind!

—*Diane Diviney Rangen*

Marlaina's Message

The most unusual incident involving my cat Marlaina happened while I was away one weekend at a conference. My usual cat-sitter was unavailable, so I let Marlaina have the run of my apartment and left her extra food and water for the day I would be gone. The last thing I remembered before locking my place was redoing my answering machine message.

I called my phone that night from the conference, wanting to see if I had any messages. The phone rang and rang, but my machine didn't kick in. I thought to myself, "I must not have turned my machine back on," and forgot about it as I went back to the conference.

My friend called the next day to ask how the conference went. After a few rings she got a "Mmrrowr?"

My friend was rather surprised to recognize Marlaina's voice on the answering machine.

"Marla?!" asked my friend.

"Mrowr," came the reply.

"Marla," my friend continued, "where's your Daddy?"

"Beeeeeep . . ." came the reply.

Marlaina had reset my answering machine and left her own outgoing message! When I came home later on, my friend left the message: "Hart, I think your cat redid your message and was rather upset you weren't home."

Since that time Marlaina has always gone with me or I've found someone to cat-sit her. We think she was trying to call out for a shrimp-and-tuna pizza, but can't prove it.

—*Hartriono Sastrowardoyo*

The Feinting Cat

As a medical editor at a large metropolitan newspaper, I thought I immediately recognized the classic symptoms: lethargy bordering on coma, frequent urination, vomiting and diarrhea, lack of appetite, high fever.

It seemed clear that Snowflake, our eight-month-old flame-point Siamese cat, was dying.

His condition triggered a flashback to 1987, when our seventeen-year-old cocker-lab-mutt, Woody, was succumbing to old age. Each night, I would carry his fading forty-pound body from our bedroom down a flight of stairs and deposit him outside our suburban Washington, D.C., house so he could do his business.

It was sad, but there was something about Woody— some crafty, diabolical streak—that gave me some hope for Snowflake.

Woody, to be blunt, was a con artist. Every time my wife and I would go on a trip, we would get a call from the house-sitter to the effect of: "Hi. Um, I think your dog is dying. He keeps collapsing during our walks, and he won't eat."

The first half dozen times this happened, we would catch the first plane home, only to be greeted by a curiously rejuvenated Woody—leaping, tail wagging, and—I swear—chuckling. After a while, our returning house-sitters (and those were becoming a rare breed), shunned the bleating canine mass at their feet as if he were trying to steal their beer while saying, "I love you, man."

Woody's Oscar-winning performance was yet to come, however. In September 1987, I was on an ill-conceived golf vacation in Florida. My wife, none too pleased about my trip to begin with, called me with the standard house-sitter line: "Your dog is dying," she said. "Maybe you'd better get off the golf course and come home." Having good reason to be skeptical, I called Woody's longtime vet, who had much less reason to ruin my vacation than did my wife or dog. "It's true," he told me. "This really seems to be it. We can keep him alive till you get home, but then I think it's time to . . ."

So, as soon as my plane landed, I rushed to the vet. Woody was carried from his cage on a type of platter. When he was placed before me in the examining room, he wasn't moving—he hadn't in several days, I was told; his eyes were cast down. I leaned down to say my last good-bye: "It's me, Woody," I whispered in his ear. "I love you, man."

Slowly, his eyes lifted toward me, he sniffed and then abruptly sprang to his feet, leaped off the examining table, and peed on the floor. Then he barked, loudly, wagged his tail, and walked to the front door. "I've never seen anything like this," said the vet. "I guess you can . . . take him home."

Woody would die two months later, but with the satisfaction of knowing he'd gotten the best of us one last time.

A couple of months ago, as Snowflake lay motionless on our dining room floor, I found myself hoping he was "pulling a Woody." But there were several things working against this: He was young and had never been out of the house, whereas Woody was world wise. As a young dog, he ran away from home and eventually showed up at a police station forty miles away; he also disappeared any number of times with the female of the species before sauntering home when he felt like it. Poor little Snowflake could never dream of such things.

The Flakester, as we call him, also has a lengthy medical history that has brought him close to death more than once. Part of a litter of a dozen, he and three siblings were discarded shortly after birth by their mother, who wanted to concentrate on feeding the hardier of her babies. Only round-the-clock hand rearing and bottle feeding by my wife and son and daughter kept Snowflake alive.

So, when we brought him to the vet in his recent condition, it was natural to think this chronically sick kitten just might be finally succumbing to his early-life traumas. But what came next was nothing short of a plot line for *ER*.

The vet's diagnosis was a surprise: diabetes. And so began the twice-daily insulin shots and special diet. Still, there was little improvement, and our worst fears returned.

After a string of lengthy and expensive hospital stays, Snowflake's enigmatic condition drove our vet to cyberspace. He consulted, via the Internet, a noted Cornell University expert, who said that Snowflake's was a special—possibly transient—case of diabetes and that we needed to switch to a different kind of insulin.

It worked wonders. The Flakester began bounding around the house (à la Woody), eating, and keeping down his food.

Then, about a week ago, the vomiting and diarrhea returned. By phone, the vet prescribed Pepcid AC. It didn't work. Snowflake was getting worse; and once again, we prepared for the worst.

Another visit to the vet, though, brought yet a new diagnosis: irritable bowel syndrome.

The Flakester has apparently dodged another bullet and is on a new regimen of antidiarrheal medicine and prescription food.

Last night, as he hopped up on the bed and settled between my wife and me, he purred for the first time in a while. And I could have sworn I heard him chuckle.

—*Joel Greenberg*

Ped's Village

We have a male silver tabby Manx named Peddler. "Ped" was an abandoned stray we rescued one bitter cold winter day at Peddlers Village in Lahaska, Pennsylvania.

He now owns us and our one-acre property. He will not tolerate another four-legged thing in our yard. Our vet bill of seventy-two dollars was evidence of an altercation with a groundhog.

Ped particularly dislikes dogs. A neighbor at the end of our street walks his large dog daily around the block. Evidently, Ped and dog had words as to who owned the street in front of our house.

The dog's master now walks him to the edge of our acre, throws the leash over his shoulder, tucks the pooper-scooper under his arm, picks up his dog, and carries him 220 feet until he is well past our grounds. Should he dare put him down too soon, Peddler will sit on the porch rail, behind bushes, and ambush the dog in passing.

The neighborhood is now Ped's Village.

—*Mary Thoman*

The Barn Cat

We pulled in the driveway that evening after visiting my grandmother at the retirement home, carrying leftovers. Grandmother wasted nothing, especially food. Anything she didn't eat she saved for us. Please understand, she didn't want us to eat these scraps; they were for our pets: two dogs and a cat. And the animals appreciated her thoughtfulness.

On this particular evening, salmon croquettes were served for dinner at the retirement home. Evidently they didn't go over too well, because Grandma had a bag of about a dozen for us. It was late February and very chilly, so we had the car windows up and the heater on as we drove home. Our goody bag, in the heat and close quarters, began to smell increasingly fishy.

As we opened the doors to get out, we unleashed all of this trapped, warm, salmon-soaked air into the cool winter evening. Within seconds, a cat ran up to us, meowing at the brown paper bag my wife was holding. Neither of us had ever seen this animal before; it was a typically marked gray and white and singularly unattractive. That is to say, ugly. It was, however, hungry.

"Give her one of those things," I said to my wife.

She dropped a croquette on the ground. The cat almost inhaled it. My wife put down two or three more, with the same results.

The cat followed us to the door. "Give it some more," I suggested. We ended up emptying the whole contents of the bag, and the cat ate every croquette.

I guess it was no surprise when the cat greeted me the next morning as I headed toward the barn. The barn is a good hike from the house; on rainy or particularly cold days, I would drive there. This morning I was going to town, so I got into the car. To my astonishment, the cat jumped in with me. The fact that the car still smelled like a fish factory may have been an incentive.

In my experience, before and since, cats are *not* good car travelers. I don't know if it's the motion or the noise or what, but they don't like it. Our house cat, for example, would stand in my lap with her front feet on my chest and her nose on mine and howl until the ride was over. This cat, however, just sat on the seat beside me and rode quietly.

I got out at the barn; the cat got out at the barn. I fed the horses, turned them out, and did all that I needed to do, then went back to the car. The cat followed me. It seemed as if I had acquired a friend.

We needed a barn cat. Badly. The house cat did not think a barn was a suitable environment, and I had put off getting a kitten for fear of its safety. We had mice, which were no threat, but we had at least one rat. The first time I saw it I thought a foal had gotten into the feed room, except that we didn't have any foals that big at the time. And, I figured, if we had one rat we probably had two.

I had put out rat poison, which had helped in the past, but it didn't seem to work this time.

I took the new cat and closed it in the feed room. I would buy some cat food in town, make the barn a desirable place, and maybe the cat would stay.

That afternoon the cat was still at the barn, and a good portion of the cat food I had put out that morning was gone. I told my wife of our new resident. I picked the animal up and checked to see if the future held a spaying or a neutering. It was a female.

The next morning she greeted me at the door again. I walked to the barn this time, and she was right at my heels. When I reached the barn, I saw in the aisle about a third of a rat. Every morning, she would greet me at the door and walk or ride with me to the barn. Within ten days or so, all evidence of a rodent problem had disappeared.

She still hadn't been named. I had just been calling her Cat and she hadn't seemed to mind, so Cat she became. It was now pretty apparent she was going to stay, so the time had come to have her spayed.

But a problem arose. She was very pregnant. Oh well, I thought, we'll wean the kittens and then have it done. We'll just hope for a small litter.

About two weeks later, Cat gave birth to four very healthy kittens. She was a good provider for her children. One day, when they were about three weeks old, I found the four kittens growling and fighting over a rabbit carcass, evidently supplied by mother. It must have been quite a battle; the rabbit was every bit as big as Cat.

As time passed I found remnants of other of Cat's hunts—mice, birds, another rabbit. There was free-choice cat food at all times, but I guess Cat was a hunter at heart.

We found homes for all four kittens by the time they were six weeks old. A couple of weeks after the last one left, I took Cat into the local small animal vet. The first thing he said was, "Boy, is that an ugly cat!" Then he said, "Grant, are you sure you want to spay her now?"

"Sure. Why?"

"She's pregnant. She's about two weeks away."

Her kittens were already eight weeks old. I had long since forgotten most of what I had learned about cats in school, but my friend explained that frequently they do have a "foal heat." Obviously Cat had had one.

Well, I decided to let her have *this* litter and then spay her.

She had four more kittens this time and fed them as

she had fed the first group, with rabbits, rodents, birds —anything Cat could catch.

Again we found homes for the kittens, but it was a little more of a challenge this time. When the last one left at about eight weeks, I took her in without waiting for her milk to go totally.

"Grant, I think she's pregnant again."

Back to the barn she went, surgery put off once more, to deliver four more very vigorous offspring. And true to form, she fed them from nature's table.

One morning, though, when the kittens were a month old, I found them fighting over a chicken! A huge chicken. It was twice the size of Cat.

The people two farms down the road, about a quarter mile, kept several chickens for the eggs. I suspected they had one fewer now.

And a few days later, they had two fewer. Maybe the first one had been sick or suicidal, but it's unlikely the flock would contain two such as that. Cat was obviously killing these birds that were much bigger than she was.

The neighbors kept their chickens in a coop. I guess there was no problem in Cat gaining entrance, but I couldn't imagine how she got the huge birds out. But she did.

A few days later, while I was out front mowing along the road, my chicken-owning neighbor pulled over and stopped.

"Hi, Mr. Clark," I said.

"Howdy, Doc. You seen any foxes? I think we got foxes."

"Foxes? No, I haven't seen any. Why?"

"I've lost three or four hens in the last week."

"I'll be darned."

I guess Cat decided these were easier prey for her, all neatly penned up as they were. I talked to her about it;

and although she was always an attentive listener, I don't think she was convinced to change her ways.

The third batch of four kittens was a real test for us to find homes for. We had used up all of our friends on the two earlier litters; this time we put little notices up in markets, feed stores, and the vet's office, among other places. In time, though, all four were in the hands of loving new owners, and Cat and I were off to the clinic again.

"Guess what?" the vet said.

"No kidding," I said.

"And she's sitting on 'go' now. I bet she'll have them within three or four days."

I should have taken his bet. It was a week, but she had four again.

The first meal I found her delivering to this family was Mr. Clark's rooster. It was immense.

When the kittens were a month old, I decided on early weaning. Once more Cat and I went to the vet. This time the surgery was performed. It had to be—I was beginning to worry about the foals. Any cat that could tackle that rooster wouldn't find much of a problem with a little horse.

I picked her up that afternoon. He told me that she had been pregnant again, but only about three weeks along. A study in fertility.

But the hunting stopped. At least I saw no more evidence of her forays. Mr. Clark reported no further lost chickens. (He had been furious over his rooster.)

The last litter of four was tough. We ran newspaper ads, we announced "free kittens" on the radio, we went up to total strangers and said, "Please!" Finally they were gone.

Cat still patrols the barn, and there hasn't been a rodent problem in several years now. She still meets me at the door in the mornings. She's still ugly.

And I paid Mr. Clark for his lost chickens. I had no idea what they cost and I didn't have the courage to tell him that I knew what happened to them, so I mailed him a twenty-dollar bill anonymously.

—Grant Kendall

The Adventures of Bubba

Our dream house had sat vacant for two years before we bought it. When we moved in, with great anticipation, we discovered that sometimes the best things in life are right at home. Certainly it was true with the big, fat, long-haired purring kitty who came to my husband and me—from right under our front steps.

Big Fat had been born to a wild mother cat who denned in a space that had been washed out right under our front concrete steps and grew up outside. When she was pushing seventeen pounds, we couldn't resist her anymore and brought her home. There was something about her size, personality, and lawn-mower purr that made us laugh.

Our last name is Butz, so Dan and I named her Big Fat, short for her full name—Big Fat Butz.

As soon as we realized Big Fat Butz was ours for good, I took her to the veterinarian to have her spayed. At the front desk, I informed the young assistant that my Big Fat Butz was six months old, had cared for all the other kittens, and I knew she was a female, since she had little milkers on her chest confirming her gender without any doubt.

The girl asked me to wait while she spoke with the doctor. I went to browse around the store part of the pet complex. It wasn't long until I heard a rather agitated voice bellowing out my cat's name: "Big Fat Butz, please!" Meekly I approached the counter to confirm that yes, I was the owner of the female cat Big Fat.

"How do you know the cat is female?" he asked.

"Oh, simple," I said, "by the little milkers on her chest!"

The vet then went on to ask if I was married? "Yes" I replied.

"Well," the vet asked, "does your husband have little milkers?"

"Well, I guess he does," I responded.

The vet went on to explain all cats and humans have those little milkers.

Big Fat as I found out that day was in fact a male cat and would be neutered rather than spayed. The vet also suggested we change the name from Big Fat to something more fitting a proud tom.

Thus Bubba was born. True to his mistaken sexual identity, Bubba was the funniest cat I've ever known.

Bubba cat was always curious about the bathtub, often jumping up and sitting on the side when anyone bathed. One night as I had washed my hair in the bathtub, I lay back to rinse out the shampoo. Bubba saw my exposed stomach and jumped down on it. It scared me, and when I screamed he leaped out. Needless to say I received a few scratches on several body parts to be left unnamed. This was the last time he tried a "Bubba bath."

That first summer Bubba was out scouting for a place to take care of his daily activities. The ground was so hard that Bubba was unable to power-dig an adequate receptacle for his deposit. After scratching and not being able to move the packed dirt, nature was making a final call and Bubba had to go. A few seconds later I noticed Bubba was carrying pieces of wood bark in his mouth to an undisclosed area. Because Bubba couldn't bury his doo-doo, he built quite an attractive monument with decorative yard bark. A few days later when my husband was out mowing the lawn, not paying any attention to the monument, he ran over it with the lawn mower. The blades went around and the bark went flying through the air, and it was no longer a mystery what Bubba had done with the bark. "Phew!"

One hot summer night we were sleeping in our secondary master suite in our basement because it was so much cooler than our bedroom. About four in the morning I heard Bubba's muffled meowing at the window, and in his mouth was the biggest dead rat I had ever seen. I refused to let Bubba come in with his prize, and he eventually left. Later that day, I checked Bubba's water and food dish, which were on our upper deck, and on top of the dried cat food he had placed the dead rat. The most amusing part was that he had carried the dead rodent up a wooden post to the second-story deck where his cat dish was located. This gave true meaning to the words *food storage*.

On a cooler summer night, we were back in our second-story master bedroom, which has a sliding glass door to the deck. We left the glass door open at night so Bubba, often out cruising most of the night, could climb up the deck post to the second story and retire on the bed without yowling to come in at 5:00 A.M. loud enough to wake the dead. On this summer night, I remember hearing my husband mumbling that Bubba was on his side of the bed, which was an unacceptable act. I wondered how this could be, because at that very time Bubba was doing his nightly routine on my feet before curling up on *my* side of the bed. I then heard a strange animal noise and I realized Bubba was not alone. I shrieked, "Someone is here!"

My husband jumped out of bed, grabbed a flashlight, and shined it brightly into the surprised eyes of our neighbor's Siamese cat, Meow Morgan. Dan yelled, I screamed, and Meow Morgan ran through the open sliding glass door, never to return.

After some discussion, we realized it was Bubba's birthday, and he was merely having a sleep-over with his closest friend.

That summer, we started noticing splattered tomatoes on our front steps and thought it must be the result of pranks by the neighborhood kids. We would clean up the tomatoes and go on our way not wanting to accuse anyone of this deed unless we were sure of the culprit.

One day we were having some work done on our house, and I came home to a rather disgruntled worker who wanted to chat with me. He went on to say he was eating his sack lunch on our front steps when our cat Bubba went after him three different times while he was eating. The guy said he finally put his lunch down, fearing for his safety. Bubba then descended on the sack and took the tomato in his mouth and ran off. I apologized and offered to replace the tomato. At that point he realized the humor of his story and started feeling a little ridiculous. He then went on to say it was really kind of cute and to forget the whole thing.

Later that day I ran into my neighbor Mrs. Hall, who said they were appalled that their tomatoes were being stolen from their back fenced yard. I didn't have the heart to tattle on my beloved Bubba cat. Alas, the mystery of her tomatoes went unsolved.

—*Janice Butz*

A Cat Is Watching

Before my daughter and her husband got their place up here near us in horse country, they owned a home on a quiet street in suburban Baltimore. Periodically, a pretty but fairly nondescript medium-coated cat appeared on their front porch or in the backyard. Eventually, she began coming into the house with the acknowledged resident cats, staying briefly only to eat or drink and even to nap a few times. She could be petted, even picked up, and was only slightly aloof. She seemed to be looking things over or thinking them through.

When my daughter checked around the neighborhood, several other families were having the same experience with the wanderer. She slept first in one house and then another, ate where she felt like eating, and was so pleasant that no one seemed to mind. Then one day she checked into my daughter and her husband's place carrying bag and baggage, and that was that. She began using the inside cat box as her regular comfort station and showed no inclination to visit old friends up and down the block. She never left the house and yard again; and when it came time to move, Lilly, her family name now, went along. The new place is apparently fine with her, too.

Clearly, Lilly was checking out what the neighborhood had to offer, and she chose well. She is, by the way, a delightful cat. When you see her curled up by the fire or on the foot of my granddaughter's bed or rubbing up against Fontine, the collie, or Zack, the Labrador retriever, purring, you have to grant her her survival skills.

I know of a more surprising case three thousand miles away in a very different world, Brentwood, just west of Beverly Hills. There has occurred a stunning victory for catkind.

Charlie and Jane Powell were children of Manhattan. They were both raised in the heart of New York City, in apartments, the children of two non-animal-oriented families, although they were culturally enriched in all other ways. There is nothing wrong with that (I guess), but it does create a kind of person who will very often stay in and repeat that mold.

Then came Mel, and it became evident that he would have to be an only child. Jane and Charlie, he a motion picture executive and she a book editor, were well read enough to know how much a pet was supposed to mean to a child, especially an only child; and although it was not a concept they knew by instinct or from firsthand experience, they decided to do what they were sure was right. Mel was to be denied nothing. With absolutely no more personal enthusiasm for the job than they would have experienced contracting a diaper service, they bought a puppy, an easy keeper for an apartment, a vest pocket–size Yorkshire terrier, Little Nell. Before they quite realized what had happened they were in love, and deeply so. They did not feign amazement, they *were* amazed! As it turned out, they had both been closet animal lovers all along, without either of them having the remotest clue that he or she was carrying the bug. It was a joy to behold. Those of us who had grown up with animals just nodded knowingly and watched the pleasant scene unfold.

In good time the inevitable call from Hollywood came, and the Powells, with Mel and Nell in tow, headed west. After Little Nell met an unexpected and unhappy fate in a freak accident, there was another Yorkie who managed to live out a good, full life. Before a third dog could be selected, something happened that changed everything. It was as unanticipated as their adoration of Little Nell. Somewhere high in the clouds a finger or perhaps a paw was pointed downward toward a beautiful house in Brentwood, and the Powells were chosen.

Their very nice home with its swimming pool and manicured gardens was being cased by a dark and handsome but secretive stranger. Day and night, we must surmise, he who was to become known as Seymour moved through their shrubbery and among their flower beds. Seymour-to-be was a black tomcat whose origins and early experiences are the secrets of the gods of the cats and not knowable. Eventually, Seymour let himself be seen and then he began to hang around in the open near the patio. Well, the Powells reckoned, the swimming pool water, full of chemicals as it always is, can't be good for a cat, so a bowl, a cut-glass bowl, a once-upon-a-time wedding present, as I recall, was put out, and the water was changed several times a day. A small enough comfort to offer a stranger perhaps from out of town.

Then one day Jane was shopping and passed the pet food aisle in the supermarket. Why not? She bought the most expensive brand of cat food they had to offer and some toys. Again, why not? So Seymour, now duly dubbed thus, was eating and drinking just outside the sliding patio doors. What happened next was inevitable. Someone en route to or from the pool left a slider slightly ajar and Seymour the moocher stepped inside never to leave again. He found a nicely puffed-up chair with a pleasing view and settled in. Then came the cat box, the litter, more toys, and a visit to the veterinarian. *Voilà!* The Powells with renewed amazement realized they adored cats, too. They hadn't had even a clue, not a tic or a murmur before Seymour joined the family.

Seymour's arrival was even more remarkable than the Powells realized. For a cat to survive in that particular area is close to miraculous. In the surrounding hills and valleys there is a great deal of urban wildlife, including plenty of coyotes who love a good haunch of domestic cat for lunch. There are feral dogs, of course, but even worse for cats are the many estates that have guard dogs on patrol off lead. The Powells' home is only about four long city blocks north of Sunset Boulevard; and that wagon track is suicidal to cross in anything less than a tank and so, for that matter, are the avenues and streets that cross and feed into it. For Seymour to have spent any time at all as a wanderer in the Brentwood Westwood area and to have achieved his adulthood was amazing.

Before Charlie and Jane could totally understand what had happened to them, Katt appeared just as Seymour had. Katt is another jet black male cat and a very handsome beast, too. The only way he can be distinguished from Seymour is by his golden eyes. Seymour's are distinctly green. Heaven only knows where Katt came from or how he survived either, but there he is in the house living as high as Seymour is, both of them in peace and harmony. Some months later another cat I never met appeared, but quickly succumbed to what the veterinarian assured Charlie and Jane was a wholly intractable urinary disorder.

Then, suddenly, Arby appeared. She is a marmalade job, about the same size as the boys, and just as pleasant. They are all remarkable moochers. Before the Powells had quite understood that they owned three cats when neither of them had ever dreamed that they would own even one, they somehow got shanghaied into a shelter and adopted their first kitten, a remarkable tortoiseshell named Moca.

Had word gotten around? Could there be an underground signal system that puts the news out, "Good pickings over on Homewood Way"? Or is it possible that cats really are watching that carefully and know or find out for themselves where the easy touches are to be found?

Several remarkable things have apparently occurred there in Brentwood. The cats, one at a time, for they came singly and spaced, picked the Powell household, although initially there was no odor of other cats to attract even Seymour. They could not possibly have belonged to the estate's previous owner, because the Powells had been in place almost twenty years before cat number one fingered them. These cats are the descendants of wild, solitary creatures, and society does not come easily or naturally to them. Many domestic cats simply cannot share a home with other cats. Yet the Powell cats, obviously masters at adaptation, snuggle up with each other to sleep, share food dishes, bathe each other, and sit around and watch each other play with stuffed mice and myriad other toys. They have adjusted themselves perfectly to obtain and retain a luxurious lifestyle, not unlike that of the rich and famous.

There had to be a waiting and watching period with

each of the three wanderers now on deck. They went shopping for people, found them, converted them (relatively easy was the conversion of the family; it had already been demonstrated they are an easy mark), and made their oh so feline deal—beauty, love, and tranquility in exchange for a world of unending luxury and devotion. Cats play for high stakes, and the Powells have bought the package. All of this displays not only feline intelligence and adaptability but the cat's power to wait, watch, and select. Selectivity without observation is the wildest of wild gambling chances. Too often with cats it has been pick right or die.

My wife, Jill, and I were recently house guests in the feline manor in Brentwood; and the morning we left for the airport I called to Jane from the drive: "Arby is out here in the bushes."

"No she's not. She's right here eating."

But there was a big marmalade cat out there, back in the bushes, just sitting and watching, and, I am sure, waiting. The Powells don't stand a chance.

—*Roger A. Caras*

Rainbo

She was a summer cat who came to us in summer dreams and lazy warm days. I spent that summer in Iowa visiting my mother—my daughter was with me—and we ended up getting a kitten that we had fallen in love with. Rainbo was her name. Every morning my daughter would take a shower and, being eight years old, would never dry off, just bounce into the living room and sit down in a rocker, hair all dripping. Every morning, Rainbo would see her dripping hair and attack that wet head—it was hilarious.

When we left Iowa to come back home to Colorado we brought Rainbo with us. Now it was time to turn Rainbo, our summer kitten, into a responsible home cat. When we stopped for gas, we put Rainbo on a leash and walked her.

When we got home, we introduced Rainbo to her new house. We have a fenced yard but we were afraid Rainbo would run away. So we put her on a long lead attached to a tree in the front yard. We gave Rainbo two weeks to get used to her yard. She spent many hours quietly scoping out the animals of the neighborhood.

When the big day came, we let her loose, hoping she wouldn't run away. We went about our daily routine of planning the day, house cleaning, breakfast, and lunch, checking outside on Rainbo every once in a while.

After a few hours someone knocked on our door. It was a neighbor from across the street who has two cats. Rainbo had strolled right in their front door, had used their cat box, and had come running back out.

I guess we forgot to show her where her cat box was located!

—*Sheryl Gray*

Beware of Dumb-Dumb

As the intruder crept into the garage of the Carter family in South Wichita, Kansas, the cat and the dog both saw him at once. Dumb-Dumb, the Carters' black cat, and Che-Che, the family's Chihuahua, shared space in the garage.

The robber froze in midstep, bracing for one of his worst nightmares: a barking—or worse, attacking—dog. But to his astonishment, the Chihuahua, a notoriously noisy breed, calmly raised her head and settled back to rest with nary a peep. The robber quietly put his hand on the knob of the door leading to the kitchen, where Mrs. Carter was working. He paid no attention to Dumb-Dumb, the cat, who bristled and arched her back on a shelf behind the man.

As the robber opened the door, Dumb-Dumb leaped into the air and landed with a furious clawhold on the man's head. The robber howled and whirled frantically, knocking over shelves in the garage, ripping the cat off his head.

Alarmed, Mrs. Carter opened the door and watched, astonished, as Dumb-Dumb sprang back onto the intruder's head, digging her claws even more deeply into his neck and cheeks, biting fiercely onto his ear and holding on.

The man hurtled screaming out of the garage and ran from the yard, blood steaming down his neck, Dumb-Dumb still clawing onto his head.

To Mrs. Carter's great relief, Dumb-Dumb returned a short while later, unharmed and as friendly as ever.

Dumb-Dumb's heroics earned him a national award for bravery, his own engraved silver feeding bowl, and a sign posted as a warning on the Carter property: "Beware of Dumb-Dumb."

—*From* **Real Animal Heroes**,
by Paul Drew Stevens
(adapted by Michael Capuzzo)

Keystone Cats

Cats understand more of what we say than we give them credit for. I've loved many cats, but never known any as clever as Pearl or Skittles. They took communication between human and feline to a new level one night. . . .

Since my husband worked the swing shift, it was our custom to save doing the dishes until after he got home from work and had his late dinner. Then we would turn on the dishwasher and go to bed, locking our two cats, Pearl and Skittles, from the bedroom (as they tended to do the fandango on our bed, and us, around 5:00 every morning). They never seemed to mind being cast out of our bedroom at night, until this one night.

We had turned on the dishwasher and gone to bed as usual, locking the cats out into the main house. After a few minutes Pearl came up to our bedroom door and started yowling. I thought this was strange, since she had never done that before, but dismissed it and hollered at her to be quiet. She ran off down the hall, and I rolled over and tried to get to sleep. A minute later Pearl was back at our door, yowling again, and scratching on the door. Again I hollered at her to go away, and again she ran off down the hall. I didn't have time to roll over before Pearl was back at the door yowling, scratching and throwing her body into the door. That did it for me.

I jumped out of bed and threw open the bedroom door to really give Pearl a good scolding. She shot off down the hall with me in hot pursuit. I thought I'd probably end up chasing her all around the house, but tripped over her as she came to a dead stop in front of the kitchen sink.

When I turned on the light I saw our other cat, Skittles, sitting on the edge of the sink watching the dishwater backing up to the top of the sink, ready to overflow onto the floor.

Omigosh, the drain's clogged! I thought as I quickly stopped the dishwasher and unclogged the drain. Pearl had been trying to tell us something was wrong. When she had run off down the hall, she had gone back to Skittles to see how the water was doing in the sink, and then come running back to our door to more urgently notify us of the problem!

I petted and praised the little fuzzies and gave them some kibble treats, turned the dishwasher back on and went back to bed—no other incidents that night.

But the next night I again turned the dishwasher on before going to bed. And again, we had been in bed only a few minutes before Pearl was again at our door yowling. This time I jumped up right away and ran down the hall after her—only this time she did not go to the kitchen. She went into the living room! Well, I checked the sink first—no problem, everything draining fine. When I turned the corner into the dark living room I immediately saw the problem. Pearl was standing in the dark staring up at the stereo. I had forgotten, for the first time, to turn off the stereo, and its little red L.E.D. power-on notification light was glowing in the dark.

I turned off the stereo (and thus the L.E.D. light), praised and petted the kitties again, gave them some more kibble treats, and went back to bed to no further incidents that night. Those were the last plumbing or electrical emergencies Pearl and Skittles figured were important enough to wake us up. After that, our house inspectors allowed us to sleep happily ever after in peace. Thank you, Lord.

—*Julie Ehmke*

The Guest

My cat, Mia, has a kitty window for her to come and go outside as she pleases. Then one day, sharing Mia's dinner, was a very large black cat. Before long, the big black tom was a regular visitor at our house, dining with Mia. So I put a collar on him with this note:

"Who am I and where do I live? I eat at Mia's house."

Two days later, I saw a note on the cat, which said:

"My name is Eclipse and I like to eat with nice neighbors like you who will feed me."

Eclipse is over every afternoon, and now he takes a nap on my chair. I still don't know where he lives, but he knows where I live.

—Carol Gallo

Lotus Blossom

This is a family story that took place about 1960. It has been retold by friends and family hundreds of times over the years. I hope you enjoy it, too.

Once upon a time our home was ruled by a beautiful Siamese cat named Lotus Blossom. She was tolerant of our family but not friendly to strangers. Visitors never made more than one attempt to pick her up. We dismissed this character flaw by saying she was a one-family cat, and we loved her dearly. To us she was a real darling, just misunderstood.

Lotus took great pleasure in slipping out of doors without being detected. Perhaps it was her way of reminding us that she was smarter than we were. My husband, Dick, and I lived in a quiet residential neighborhood in Barrington, New Jersey, but I was always concerned when Lotus was outside—not only for her but for anyone who might cross her path. I could usually find her by checking the backyards on both sides of DuBois Avenue.

One morning, after Dick had left for work, I realized Lotus was not in the house. I followed my usual search route without success. It was a lovely, brisk fall day. Brightly colored leaves covered the ground and were heaped at curbside, a wonderful camouflage for a mischievous Siamese. I went out to look for her several more times, and I telephoned a few neighbors to put them on alert. I finally went back to my ironing, but I couldn't concentrate on it.

At noon the doorbell rang. As I opened the door an enormous shape filled the entryway. This was unmistakably a truck driver; heavy boots, work clothes, a very formidable-looking fellow. He was holding a large brown bag rather gingerly in front of him. In a gruff voice he said, "Lady, do you own a Siamese cat?"

My heart stopped; I couldn't breathe, couldn't say a word. In an instant I visualized how it must have happened: Lotus hiding in the leaves by the curb when this man pulled up in his very large truck. I was sure our beloved Lotie was in that bag, crushed! Bracing myself for the inevitable, I managed to nod, "Yes."

"Well," he growled, "your cat ate my lunch!" And he opened his bag to show me what was left of his sandwich. I couldn't believe it! Our Lotus was still alive out there somewhere. When the man went to his truck (left with the windows open) for his bag lunch, there was Lotus and what was left of his meal. Lotus had fled without an introduction, but a neighborhood witness identified the cat as ours. This man was obviously upset —and hungry! Fortunately we had had company for dinner the night before, and I was able to make him several leftover roast beef sandwiches and include a generous slice of cake. As the trucker left he seemed quite satisfied with his substitute lunch, but I prayed his path and Lotus's wouldn't cross again.

Lotus came home a few hours later, inscrutable as always, apparently unruffled by the events of the day, lips sealed.

—*Shirle Collings and Mary Jane Pentz*

Feeding the Dog

I was bathing peacefully in a hot tub when I heard my husband laugh. I didn't think much of it because he was watching the television. When he laughed again, I said, "That must be a real funny movie you're watching." His reply brought me from the comfort of my bath to a quick wrap of a towel. "Watch the cat," he said.

Nicholas (the cat) jumped up on my kitchen counter. I keep a plastic container with dog bones up there for Jabip, our female pit bull. With his head Nicholas removed the container top and bit one of the bones. Lifting the bone gently with his teeth he placed it on the counter. Meanwhile my dog was sitting pretty below him, waiting very patiently. Nicholas pushed the bone very slowly and carefully with his paw, inching it to the end of the counter. He stopped there and looked down at the dog for about ten seconds, then pushed the bone overboard!

We could hardly believe our eyes, and laughed in disbelief. Every day our pit bull licks the cat's head for approximately ten minutes as Nicky stretches his legs in enjoyment. Maybe Nicky is returning the favor!

—Lisa and John Ermine

Feeding the People

Some cats think humans are terrible hunters and would surely starve without their assistance. Often, help comes in the form of a dead mouse. My mother-in-law's beautiful black cat did it differently. Every morning, she carried a fresh loaf of bread in her mouth and left it on our windowsill. This went on for a while until we realized it wasn't the bread driver leaving it at the wrong house. The cat was stealing it from a neighbor's windowsill and bringing it to us. The driver caught her doing it.

—Ruth Schneer

Showering Sage

Karen grew up in a house with three kids and one bathroom. She dreamed of the day when she could shower in peace. Someday, she would luxuriate alone in the warm, soothing water. No one would rudely bang on the bathroom door.

"Finally, I live by myself in my own house," she said. "It has two bathrooms for one person—but I still have to share."

He's an absolute animal, too, demanding to get in the water with her. Karen showers with her fifteen-pound cat, Sage.

I am sorry this interspecies scrub is not a complete success. "He hogs the hot water and stands in the way," Karen said.

If you're not a cat owner, take my word for it: Water-loving cats are rare. The average cat likes water about as much as the average kid likes broccoli. Cat lovers claim felines are clean animals, in spite of their aquatic aversion. They say cats are more tidy and less smelly than dogs. They point out that cats constantly lick their fur. I'm not sure spit baths are a sign of superior hygiene. Consider what cats use for toilet paper.

Anyway, there's nothing else unusual about Sage. He is an ordinary striped tomcat who lives in Maryville, Illinois. He didn't develop his strange affinity for water until age twelve.

"It makes no sense at all," Karen said. "The few times I tried to give him a bath, he fought me. When he scratched me near my eye, I never tried to bathe him again."

Then Karen came home one day and found water all over the bathroom floor. She tried to put a lid on this behavior by keeping the commode closed.

"But sometimes a visitor would leave it up. One evening, when the house was quiet, I heard *splish splish* . . . *splish splish*. I tiptoed around the corner to spy my cat standing on the rim of the commode, playing in the water. There was water everywhere. It looked like he was trying to scoop it all out."

Plenty of pets will dog paddle in the commode. That doesn't mean they wind up sharing your shower. But for Sage, it was a small step from the porcelain pond to the waterfall.

"Shortly after that, I was taking a shower. He pulled the shower curtain open with his paw and peeked in. The next time I looked down, he was completely in the shower. Sage was batting at the water with his paw and licking it like it was some kind of huge water fountain. He was drenched. And he liked it."

How does he dry off?

"That's the bad part. He gets out and lies on my bed —soaking wet—until he dries. I shoo him off, but he goes back as soon as I leave."

Karen figured his interest would eventually dry up. She figured wrong.

"He's obsessed with his daily shower experience. Now he gets into the shower before I do and calls me to get the water running. He's in there every morning, meowing."

If Karen shuts him out of the bathroom to shower alone, "he will knock on the door until I let him in. I have actually taken advantage of this to bathe him. He's so preoccupied with the water that he doesn't know he's getting a bath until I have him lathered up, and then it's too late."

Recently, Sage expanded his territory. Now he claims the bathroom sink as his watering hole. "When I brush my teeth, I have to battle for the faucet. I was soaking something in the sink, and he pulled it out and splashed the water all over. Anywhere he hears running water, he's there.

"Even though I'm living alone, I'm still sharing the bathroom. And not just with my cat. My dog has to use the hair dryer every morning. But that's another story. . . ."

—Elaine Viets

The Feline Scorned

Cats teach us many timeless lessons, not the least of which is this: Beware the woman scorned. Our cat, Olivia, for instance, believes that she really is my husband's master. She loves him very much, but she rules him with an iron fist.

One late evening when we all retired, we climbed into bed to watch the news. Olivia, of course, took her rightful place at my husband's side, laying her head next to his on the pillow and her body in the crook of his arm. This is how he is supposed to spend the whole night sleeping. When he tired of this and turned over she followed him to the other side. Not wanting to continue on with this sleeping arrangement, my husband put the pillow over his head. Olivia, not to be daunted, tried to burrow under the pillow. When she could not succeed she sat down in contemplation for a minute, deciding what to do. Ever so calmly she walked around to the other side of the bed and very deliberately walked along his side until she reached his derriere. There she stopped, promptly and with vigor gave him a firm bite on his posterior as reprimand! Beware the woman scorned . . . she walks softly but carries a big bite.

—*Anne H. Timpson*

Johnny Cat

Several years ago, a cat had a litter of kittens in my back shed. When she found out I knew they were there she carried them off but left one and never came back for him. After a few days of listening to him crying, I felt sorry and brought him into the house and hand-fed him. I called him Johnny Cat. Johnny was my husband's name and he hated cats. But Johnny Cat turned out to be a prophetic name in ways I never would have dreamed.

Johnny Cat followed me around while I got ready for work, always following me to the bathroom. One morning as he sat on the toilet watching me comb my hair I heard water tinkle in the toilet. I was amazed and praised Johnny Cat and flushed the toilet. I figured he did it accidentally but bragged about it to everyone.

Next morning, he did it again.

For the next nine years that I had my beautiful gray-and-white Johnny Cat he used the toilet every time. He had no privacy at all because when he headed for the bathroom someone always peeked around the corner to watch him. Some people thought I was crazy until I showed them pictures I took or brought them in the house to show them. I just wish I could have taught him to flush.

—*Betty Flores*

CHAPTER SIX

Universal Love

I have been scientifically studying the traits and dispositions of the "lower animals" and contrasting them with the traits and dispositions of man. I find the result profoundly humiliating to me. For it obliges me to renounce my allegiance to the Darwinian theory of the Ascent of Man from the Lower Animals; since it now seems plain to me that that theory ought to be vacated in favor of a new and truer one, the Descent of Man from the Higher Animals.

Mark Twain

The Cat and the Gorilla

It's always hard to say good-bye. As a parish minister, part of my job is caring for the dying and bereaved, but finding the right words doesn't get any easier with practice. What do you say to the parents whose one-day-old daughter—their first child—died because she was born with part of her heart missing? What do you say at a memorial service for a forty-five-year-old man, a cancer victim, that will give solace and support to his widow and two teenagers? Words aren't adequate to address the shock and desolation we feel when a loved one dies.

The only thing that seems to help is a caring presence. So we gather with our families. Our friends come around. We assemble in our spiritual communities. We light a candle, share a hug, or join in a moment of silence. And although we don't stop grieving, we know that we don't grieve alone. Others, who have also borne tragedy in their lives, understand the pain we feel. And out of that shared suffering we somehow gather strength to endure the loss.

People in my congregation have come to me many times for counseling when their animal companions die. The loss of a beloved dog or cat can be very upsetting and naturally makes us sad. As with the death of a fellow human being, when a pet dies it's helpful not to grieve alone. But I am convinced, thanks to the remarkable relationship of a cat and a gorilla, that we as a species do not mourn life's tragedies alone—animals, also, have strong spiritual feelings and cope with feelings of loss.

Koko is a female lowland gorilla who for almost two decades has been the focus of the world's longest ongoing ape language study. Instead of using spoken words,

Koko communicates in Ameslan, or American Sign Language. Her teacher, Dr. Francine "Penny" Patterson of the California Gorilla Foundation, has helped Koko master a vocabulary of more than five hundred words. That's how Koko told Penny she wanted a cat for her birthday. She signed the word *cat* by drawing two fingers across her cheeks to indicate whiskers.

When Koko requested a cat of her own, she was given a concrete statue that she kissed and rubbed against her cheek. She treated it so gently that one day, six months later, one of her caretakers brought three kittens to the rural compound in Woodside, California, where Koko lives. The kittens had been abandoned at birth. Their "foster mother" was a cairn terrier who suckled them through the first month of life.

Koko looked down at the kittens and signed, "Love that."

Handling them with the gentle behavior typical of gorillas, Koko chose her pet, a tailless kitten with gray fur. She named her young friend "All Ball."

Koko enjoyed her new kitten for six blissful months, sniffing it and stroking it tenderly. When the kitten purred, so did the gorilla: a deep, throaty rumble. Koko combed All Ball's head, fed him her luncheon lettuce, carried All Ball tucked against her upper leg and attempted to nurse it as if it were a baby gorilla, signing, "You mouth nipple." Koko was surprised to learn that kittens bite. When All Ball bit her on the finger, she made the signs for "dirty" and "toilet," her usual expressions of disapproval. It wasn't long, though, before Koko was signing the cat to tickle her—one of the gorilla's favorite games. "Koko seems to think that cats can do most things that she can do," said Penny. "Soft/good/cat," said Koko.

One night All Ball escaped from the Gorilla Foundation and was accidentally killed by a car. Patterson told

Koko, speaking in a trembling voice as she signed, "He was hit by a car. We won't be seeing him anymore." Koko acted as if she didn't hear or understand. Then a few minutes later she started to cry with high-pitched sobs—the same cry she made as an infant when Patterson left her for the night.

Koko's grief was shared by her people.

"When she started whimpering, a distinct hooting sound that gorillas make when they are sad," said microbiologist Ronald Cohn, Patterson's companion, "we all started crying together."

For nearly a week after the loss Koko cried when the subject of cats came up. "Sad/frown" and "Sleep/cat" were her responses when the kitten was mentioned later.

The gorilla clearly missed her cat. But how much did she understand about what had happened? Fortunately, it was possible to ask Koko directly. Maureen Sheehan, a staff member at the Gorilla Foundation, interviewed Koko about her thoughts on death.

"Where do gorillas go when they die?" Maureen asked.

Koko replied, "Comfortable/hole/bye [the sign for kissing a person good-bye]."

"When do gorillas die?" she asked.

Koko replied with the signs "Trouble/old."

"How do gorillas feel when they die: happy, sad, afraid?"

"Sleep," answered Koko.

The awareness of death is what makes human life so bittersweet and poignant. There is much evidence that we are not alone in this regard.

For two months, Koko gave every indication of being in mourning. In quiet moments she sobbed, though less often. She received piles of condolence mail, much of it from children, who did not think it strange that a gorilla should be capable of feelings that had been attributed only to humans.

As anyone who has lost a pet knows, mourning is a highly individual thing. The urge to love and be loved is so strong many people welcome another pet into their lives. Others take years to reach that stage or, sadly, never achieve it.

Asked what she wanted for Christmas, Koko hesitantly signed, "Cat/cat/tiger/cat." When Patterson appeared with a yellow male Manx kitten in her pocket, Koko was so excited she spun around on her knuckles.

Koko cradled the kitten in her arms and signed, "Baby."

—*Gary Kowalski*

The Cat and the Bear

The orange kitten was hungry. The grizzly bear was lonely. The man was apprehensive.

"This cat weighed no more than ten ounces when he slid under the fence into the bear's pen," says Dave Siddon, founder of Wildlife Images, an animal rehabilitation center in Grants Pass, Oregon. "I was almost in a panic. I thought the bear would swat him and kill him. Grizzlies are omnivorous, you know. They'll eat baby fawns, baby moose, baby elk, baby beaver."

But not, as it turns out, a certain baby cat.

The grizzly, whose name is Griz, had come to the center in 1990, when he was just a cub. Hit by a train while foraging on railroad tracks in Montana, he suffered severe head injuries and was deemed unfit ever to be returned to the wild. "He's the gentlest, sweetest thing you ever saw," says Siddon. "He's sort of the Forrest Gump of bears."

The kitten, whose name now is, simply, Cat, was one of four kittens abandoned at the center early last summer. Volunteers were able to trap and find homes for the rest of the litter. But Cat somehow eluded them.

Then one day in July, Cat, about six weeks old, turned up in Griz's pen. Afraid to do anything that might alarm Griz, Siddon just watched, expecting the worst. Then, as the 650-pound grizzly was eating his midday meal—a five-gallon bucket of kibble, meat, fruit, vegetables, and road-kill venison—something extraordinary happened.

"The bear very gently picked out a chicken wing," says Siddon, "and dropped it, by his own forepaw, for the cat." The two proceeded to do lunch.

Since then, Griz and Cat have become something of a slapstick animal act. "Cat will lay in ambush, then leap out and swat Griz on his nose," says Siddon. "Sometimes, Griz carries Cat around in his mouth. Cat will ride on Griz's back. Sometimes Griz licks Cat."

Carl Jung, the great Swiss psychologist, believed there were archetypes in the collective unconscious—eternal myths in the genetic makeup of human beings that give meaning to our lives, endlessly repeating myths of the hero, the mentor, the jester, and other archetypes.

Jung believed it was possible animals, too, inherited a tendency to create archetypes of meaning.

Watching the cat and the bear play, it seems possible.

"It's almost," Siddon marvels, "as if the bear were the protector and the cat were the mischievous child."

As word of these antics has spread, the number of visitors at the nonprofit refuge has doubled, and donations have soared. But Siddon values Cat and Griz's unlikely friendship for other reasons.

"It's so pure and simple," he says, "an example of Mother Nature at her best."

—*People Weekly* **magazine**

Moses

It was going to take a definite effort of will to get out of the car. I had driven about ten miles from Darrowby, thinking all the time that the Dales always looked their coldest not when they were covered with snow but, as now, when the first sprinkling streaked the bare flanks of the fells in bars of black and white like the ribs of a crouching beast. And now in front of me was the farm gate rattling on its hinges as the wind shook it.

The car, heaterless and draughty as it was, seemed like a haven in an uncharitable world and I gripped the wheel tightly with my woolen-gloved hands for a few moments before opening the door. The wind almost tore the handle from my fingers as I got out but I managed to crash the door shut before stumbling over

the frozen mud to the gate. Muffled as I was in heavy
coat and scarf pulled up to my ears I could feel the icy
gusts biting my face, whipping up my nose and ham-
mering painfully into the air spaces in my head.

I had driven through and, streaming-eyed, was about
to get back into the car, when I noticed something
unusual. There was a frozen pond just off the path and
among the rime-covered rushes which fringed the dead
opacity of the surface a small object stood out, shiny
black.

I went over and looked closer. It was a tiny kitten,
probably about six weeks old, huddled and immobile,
eyes tightly closed. Bending down I poked gently at the
furry body. It must be dead; a morsel like this couldn't
possibly survive in such cold . . . but no, there was a
spark of life because the mouth opened soundlessly for
a second and then closed.

Quickly I lifted the little creature and tucked it inside
my coat. As I drove into the farmyard I called to the
farmer who was carrying two buckets out of the calf
house. "I've got one of your kittens here, Mr. Butler. It
must have strayed outside."

Mr. Butler put down his buckets and looked blank.
"Kitten? We haven't got no kittens at present."

I showed him my find and he looked more puzzled.

"Well, that's a rum 'un, there's no black cats on this
spot. We've all sorts o' colors but no black 'uns."

"Well, he must have come from somewhere else," I
said. "Though I can't imagine anything so small travel-
ling very far. It's rather mysterious."

I held the kitten out and he engulfed it with his big,
work-roughened hand.

"Poor little beggar, he's only just alive. I'll take him
into t'house and see if the missus can do owt for him."

In the farm kitchen Mrs. Butler was all concern. "Oh,
what a shame!" She smoothed back the bedraggled hair

with one finger. "And it's got such a pretty face." She looked up at me. "What is it, anyway, a him or a her?"

I took a quick look behind the hind legs. "It's a tom."

"Right," she said. "I'll get some warm milk into him but first of all we'll give him the old cure."

She went over to the fireside oven on the big black kitchen range, opened the door and popped him inside.

I smiled. It was the classical procedure when newborn lambs were found suffering from cold and exposure; into the oven they went and the results were often dramatic. Mrs. Butler left the door partly open and I could just see the little black figure inside; he didn't seem to care much what was happening to him.

The next hour I spent in the byre wrestling with the overgrown hind feet of a cow. Still, I thought, as I eased the kinks from my spine when I had finished, there were compensations. There was a satisfaction in the sight of the cow standing comfortably on two almost normal-looking feet.

"Well, that's summat like," Mr. Butler grunted. "Come in the house and wash your hands."

In the kitchen as I bent over the brown earthenware sink I kept glancing across at the oven.

Mrs. Butler laughed. "Oh, he's still with us. Come and have a look."

It was difficult to see the kitten in the dark interior but when I spotted him I put out my hand and touched him and he turned his head towards me.

"He's coming around," I said. "That hour in there has worked wonders."

"Doesn't often fail." The farmer's wife lifted him out. "I think he's a little tough 'un." She began to spoon warm milk into the tiny mouth. "I reckon we'll have him lappin' in a day or two."

"You're going to keep him, then?"

"Too true we are. I'm going to call him Moses."

"Moses?"

"Aye, you found him among the rushes, didn't you?"
I laughed. "That's right. It's a good name."

I was on the Butler farm about a fortnight later and I
kept looking around for Moses. Farmers rarely have
their cats indoors and I thought that if the black kitten
had survived he would have joined the feline colony
around the buildings.

Farm cats have a pretty good time. They may not be
petted or cosseted but it has always seemed to me that
they lead a free, natural life. They are expected to catch
mice but if they are not so inclined there is abundant
food at hand; bowls of milk here and there and the
dogs' dishes to be raided if anything interesting is left
over. I have seen plenty of cats around today, some
flitting nervously away, others friendly and purring.
There was a tabby loping gracefully across the cobbles
and a big tortoiseshell was curled on a bed of straw at
the warm end of the byre; cats are connoisseurs of
comfort. When Mr. Butler went to fetch the hot water
I had a quick look in the bullock house and a white tom
regarded me placidly from between the bars of a hay
rack where he had been taking a siesta. But there was
no Moses.

I finished drying my arms and was about to make a
casual reference to the kitten when Mr. Butler handed
me my jacket.

"Come round here with me if you've got a minute,"
he said, "I've got summat to show you."

I followed him through the door at the end and
across a passage into the long, low-roofed piggery. He
stopped at a pen about halfway down and pointed inside.

"Look 'ere," he said.

I leaned over the wall and my face must have shown

my astonishment because the farmer burst into a shout of laughter.

"That's summat new for you, isn't it?"

I stared unbelievably down at a large sow stretched comfortably on her side, suckling a litter of about twelve piglets, and right in the middle of the long pink row, furry black and incongruous, was Moses. He had a teat in his mouth and was absorbing his nourishment with the same rapt enjoyment as his smooth-skinned fellows on either side.

"What the devil . . . ?" I gasped.

Mr. Butler was still laughing. "I thought you'd never have seen anything like that before; I never have, any road."

"But how did it happen?" I still couldn't drag my eyes away.

"It was the missus's idea," he replied. "When she'd got the little youth lappin' milk she took him out to find a right warm spot for him in the buildings. She settled on this pen because the sow, Bertha, had just had a litter and I had a heater in and it was grand and cosy."

I nodded. "Sounds just right."

"Well, she put Moses and a bowl of milk in here," the farmer went on, "but the little feller didn't stay by the heater very long—next time I looked in he was round at t'milk bar."

I shrugged my shoulders. "They say you see something new every day at this game, but this is something I've never even heard of. Anyway, he looks well on it—does he actually live on the sow's milk or does he still drink from his bowl?"

"A bit of both, I reckon. It's hard to say."

Anyway, whatever mixture Moses was getting he grew rapidly into a sleek, handsome animal with an

unusually high gloss to his coat which may or may not
have been due to the porcine element of his diet.

I never went to the Butlers' without having a look in
the pig pen. Bertha, his foster mother, seemed to find
nothing unusual in this hairy intruder and pushed him
around casually with pleased grunts just as she did the
rest of her brood.

Moses for his part appeared to find the society of the
pigs very congenial. When the piglets curled up together and settled down for a sleep Moses would be
somewhere in the heap, and when his young colleagues
were weaned at eight weeks he showed his attachment
to Bertha by spending most of his time with her.

And it stayed that way over the years. Often he would
be right inside the pen, rubbing himself happily along
the comforting bulk of the sow, but I remember him
best in his favourite place; crouching on the wall looking down perhaps meditatively on what had been his
first warm home.

—*James Herriot*

The Cat and the Canary

Humans, as Mark Twain once noted, have too long believed that animals act only on survival instinct—and that compassion is a human characteristic, raising us above the lower orders.

The terrible story of the thirteenth-century Welsh prince Llewellyn and his brave wolfhound, Gelert, is the classic example. One day the prince was hunting, and he noticed that Gelert was not at his side. Suspicious, the prince rode home promptly and was greeted at the door by Gelert. The giant wolfhound's mouth was streaked with blood, the prince's young son's cradle was overturned, and the house was a shambles.

Surmising instantly that his favorite wolfhound had killed his son, Llewellyn drew his sword and plunged it into Gelert's heart, killing the dog instantly. Only then did he hear his son's cry from beneath the cradle, and discover the torn shape of a dead wolf in the corner of the hall. Prince Llewellyn had killed the dog who had bravely saved his son's life. From this story comes a famous Welsh proverb: To repent as deeply as the man who killed his dog.

The story of the cat and the canary indicates that, perhaps, our species is learning and growing.

A canary and a cat grew up together and became close friends. They would play together, and when the cat slept the canary perched on the sleeping cat's belly. None of the typical cat-bird animosity existed between them.

Joan, the woman in the family, came home one day and found her canary dead on the floor. Convinced her cat had finally succumbed to instinct and killed her canary, Joan screamed furiously at the cat sitting nearby and tried to swat her but the cat dashed out the door.

Later, on examining the bird, Joan realized that it

had simply died of old age; there were no teeth marks, no sign of attack whatsoever. Guiltily, she called for her cat but the falsely accused animal would not return.

The cat's habit was to come home every evening by 8:00, but this time she did not appear. As the hours passed, the woman grew more and more anxious for her falsely accused cat.

Finally at midnight, to her great relief, she heard a scratching at the door. When she opened the door, there was the cat on the threshold, delicately holding a live fledgling in her mouth. Gently the cat placed the little bird on the floor at the woman's feet, backed away, and sat down to watch her human expectantly.

The young bird blinked and peeped. The cat had obviously stolen the fledgling from its nest. The cat looked hopefully up at Joan to see if the new bird would ease her sorrow. The cat's look seemed to say, "Can we be friends again now? I've brought you another bird."

—*Stephanie Laland and Michael Capuzzo*

The Cat and the Rabbit

One winter, the cat and the rabbit slept together at our house, best of friends, curling up by the wood-burning stove. Then six little rabbits were born. . . .

Tom was a large yellow tiger cat who allowed us to live with him in Springfield, Ohio. He was a very independent fellow coming and going as he pleased. Jenny was a white, pink-eyed rabbit who shared our house, too. We were wary when we introduced them, but to our relief they accepted each other well. As time passed they seemed to have a special communication going. But as we were ignorant of cat and rabbit language we never knew what they said or how they said it.

Then one winter they communicated in a universal language even we could understand.

That winter, Jenny gave birth to six little rabbits: five white and one brown. They were born in her cage in the kitchen, and the door to the rabbit cage remained open at all times allowing Jenny the freedom to come and go from her little bunnies. However, we grew concerned as occasionally a rat would get into the house, and we were afraid for the baby rabbits.

Jenny and Tom were way ahead of us. When Jenny took a break Tom would go into the cage and the big cat would keep a protective eye on the bunnies until their mother returned. This continued until the babies were large enough to take care of themselves.

—*Sally Robbins*

A Cat's Best Friend

The year was 1990, and Philip Gonzalez was optimistic about his prospects. The forty-year-old Vietnam veteran was earning a good living as a steam fitter. Weekdays he would commute to his construction job in Manhattan and return home to his one-bedroom apartment on Long Island for a simple vegetarian dinner. He traveled, played sports, and indulged his taste in good clothes and gold jewelry. Philip might have enjoyed such modest pleasures for years to come, but a terrible accident swept it all away.

"I was putting some tools away when a big machine that cuts and threads pipe caught my right arm by the coat sleeve," he recalls. He struggled to free himself but was swept up by the rotating machine as it mangled his arm, dashing his head against the concrete floor repeatedly as it spun. He's thankful that he was unconscious through most of the ordeal.

Philip narrowly escaped amputation, but his right arm—his good arm—was all but useless. He also endured serious trauma, and the cumulative injuries left him permanently disabled, unable to work, and so broken in spirit that he refused to leave his apartment.

A concerned neighbor, Sheilah Harris, hit on an idea to restore his hope: an animal companion.

Together, Sheilah and Philip went to their local animal shelter. "I wanted a big dog," says Philip, "a rottweiler or a Doberman, but the shelter didn't have any dogs on the adoption floor that I liked." They were about to go when the attendant said he had two more dogs in the back recovering from being spayed—one of them a Doberman. Philip went to the cage; and although he had his eye on the Doberman, a strange, shepherd-sized scruffy dog came right up to the bars and started to lick his hand. Philip wasn't interested, but Sheilah implored him to take the dog for a walk around the block. To appease her, Philip agreed. By the time they returned, Philip was ready to fill out the adoption papers.

The shelter attendant told Philip that the dog, a mix of Siberian husky and schnauzer, had been found locked with her three pups in the closet of an abandoned apartment. She had been left without food or water. Her hair had fallen out from malnutrition and she was badly dehydrated but when found, she was still guarding her pups with her last bit of strength.

Moved by the story, Philip looked down at the dog to see her body wiggling with excitement and her tail wagging furiously. Despite all she'd been through, she was full of love and enthusiasm. Philip realized that as much as he thought he had to offer this dog, the dog had just as much to offer him. He promptly named the dog Ginny—after the Barbie-like dolls Sheilah collected—and brought her home, her nose tucked under his chin for the duration of the ride.

Three days after Ginny's homecoming, Philip walked her by a vacant lot. Ginny saw a cat and ran after it, her leash slipping from Philip's hand. Ginny shot toward the cat as Philip looked on helplessly, fearful that the two would fight. To his amazement, Ginny started licking and grooming the cat. The cat was purring and rubbing against Ginny so Philip let them nuzzle for about an hour before tearing the reluctant Ginny away.

As soon as they got back to the apartment, Ginny started whining to go back to the vacant lot. This time, Philip thought to grab a can of dog food to feed the cat. The cat gobbled it gratefully and played with Ginny, even riding on her back for a gallop around the lot. Philip returned every day to feed the stray but soon the "stray" turned to "strays."

"There must have been fifty cats," Philip says laugh-

ing, "and Ginny wanted to play with all of them."
Whenever Philip walked Ginny, all the cats would
come out of their hiding places and walk alongside her.
A passerby who witnessed the spectacle called out to
Philip, "What are you, the Pied Piper of Long Island?
Why are all those cats following you?"

In answer, Philip dropped the leash, letting Ginny
veer off in another direction. The cats followed Ginny,
leaving Philip standing alone.

After the experience with the cats at the vacant lot,
Philip figured that Ginny might want a cat of her own.
The two headed down to the shelter, where Philip assumed they would spend a couple of hours choosing
among the shelter's eighty-odd cats. Once again,
Ginny proved to have a mind of her own. As soon as
she was led to the cat adoption area, Ginny made a
beeline for a cage holding a white kitten. She whined
and paced in front of the cage, begging for the cat.
Philip didn't see anything special about the kitten but
he adopted it. Two days later he learned that there was
something special about the kitten Ginny chose: She
was deaf.

Philip didn't know it, but Ginny would not be satisfied with one cat. A week later, Ginny accompanied
Philip as he carried a donation of cat and dog treats to
the shelter. Again, Ginny came to a halt in front of a
cat cage. She went into her begging routine. The object of Ginny's excitement? A cat with one eye. Philip
shrugged and took it home. At a routine vet appointment, Ginny caught sight of a cat with a rope around
her neck. The vet was going to put the cat to sleep
because she had lost her rear paws to frostbite and because she was a wild, hissing cat who stood no chance
of adoption. Philip was determined not to take the cat,
but Ginny insisted. They took her home.

After this latest adoption, Philip began to suspect that

Ginny wasn't just fond of cats—she was on a mission to rescue disabled ones who might otherwise die alone. He realized that Ginny had been chosen for this work and that she had chosen him to help her complete it.

Not content to wait for cats to cross her path, Ginny began to seek them out. One day, Philip was walking Ginny by a building undergoing construction work. She insisted on going in. Philip let her off lead, and she dashed off, returning holding a cat by the scruff of its neck. When Ginny let the cat drop from her jaws, Philip saw that it was unable to walk and seemed dazed.

At first, Philip thought the cat must have fallen from a great height but a closer look revealed that the cat wasn't wounded. A trip to the vet solved the mystery: hyperplasia—a type of brain damage. The vet advised Philip to have the cat put down, but he adopted her and took her home to join the growing menagerie.

Three weeks later, Topsy, so named because she gets around by rolling from place to place, was joined by five other new additions. Ginny dragged Philip into the same abandoned building where she'd found Topsy and headed straight for a seven-foot-long, five-inch-wide section of pipe standing on its end. Ginny knocked it over and revealed five newborn kittens cowering there. They'd probably been stuffed into the pipe to die. After a flea dip at the now-familiar vet's office, all five headed for home. Philip mixed formula and fed them from a bottle; Ginny provided maternal TLC, licking them clean and sitting with them in the apartment's sole bathtub that now served as a kitten nursery.

Against the odds, every cat Philip and Ginny adopted blossomed into a loving, affectionate creature. After mere days in their care, the cats adjusted to the household's routines. At night, the cats jockey for prime real estate on top of Philip's chest and during the day, Ginny spends much of her time grooming the cats to her exacting standards. Yet while their success was boundless, Philip had to confront the fact that their space was not. The tiny apartment sheltered fifteen cats, and neighbor Sheilah sheltered an additional fifteen, but still Ginny found more. As the number of hungry little mouths kept increasing, Philip began boarding some cats with his vet. He also started to search for good homes for new arrivals. He's been tirelessly searching for more ever since.

Today, with Ginny to guide him, Philip devotes his waking hours to rescuing cats. Seven years after Ginny first found him, Philip estimates that his friend has found over 300 cats. Of these, he's found homes for 170, and he feeds another 120 cats who live outdoors. He has every cat spayed or neutered and tags the ones who live outdoors so vets who find them will know their shots are up-to-date and that they are "one of Ginny's." Philip pays for much of this out of his tiny worker's compensation check. He long ago sold his gold jewelry to buy cat food. His local veterinary office, All Creatures, helps out with greatly reduced fees, and he sometimes gets donations of cat food from people who know of his dog's passion for cats.

Recently, Philip and Ginny got a little cash boost from the sale of two books about Ginny's rescue: *The Dog Who Rescues Cats* (HarperCollins, 1995) and *Blessing of the Animals* (HarperCollins, 1996). As much as the extra dollars for cat food, Philip is grateful for the support of animal lovers. It's often hard, humbling, lonely work keeping up with Ginny, but Philip says the rescues have transformed his life.

"Ginny actually picked me for her person," marvels Philip, "perhaps because she knew I was disabled. Then she showed me, by example, how much satisfaction there is in rescuing helpless animals. She gave my life a purpose, a new kind of happiness.

"I've never known so much affection in my life as I get from my precious cats and my angelic dog. My days were empty before Ginny; now they are filled with joyous work morning and night."

Not everyone understands why he would devote himself to this cause. "Sometimes I'm asked, what kind of life is that?" Gonzalez says.

"It's my life," he answers. "And I'm happy with it. I am needed as I was never before needed in my life, by all the homeless and hungry and mistreated animals. In my old life I had plenty of fun but no real happiness. Little Ginny, part schnauzer, part Siberian husky, part angel from heaven, has taught me the most important lesson in life, that life is not worth living without love, that giving love is more rewarding than getting it, and that the humblest creatures, the least advantaged creatures, are worthy of the greatest outpouring of love. If that's not heaven's message, I'd like to know what is.

"My little Ginny is in the lifesaving business, and the first life she saved was mine."

—*Catherine Censor Shemo*

The Cat and the Baby

It's a special moment when I'm entrusted with the care of my baby grandson, Jack. One morning, I was happily sitting in my rocking chair with Jack in my arms when he started to cry. Now, as a grandmother I have plenty of experience in comforting babies, and I knew soon as his cries grew loud and insistent that Jack was hungry. Jack was ready to be nursed, but his mommy was running a few minutes late.

Soon the baby's wails drew the attention of my fourteen-year-old cat, K.C. K.C. hopped up onto the footstool next to my rocker and stared at the baby and then at me with great consternation. Over that baby's cries I explained, "K.C., the baby is hungry. His mommy will be here soon. I can't feed the baby, K.C. He's a hungry baby . . . a very hungry baby."

I didn't pay much attention when K.C. left us. He went right outside through the cat door, and I continued to rock and soothe little Jack. Within five minutes, K.C. startled me by again hopping up onto the footstool. This time with a live bird in his mouth!

I believe that K.C. was trying to soothe the hunger pangs of another mammal. I've never known K.C. to catch a bird in his life before that, or since.

—*Roxi DiSante*

CHAPTER SEVEN

Heroism

God, devil, witch, saint, sorcerer, prophet, temptress, queen of the universe, victim of the stake. Cats have worn every hat in history except, not once, the hero. Now, at last, it is their turn.

Rachel Lamb

Kimberly's Best Friend

Greg Harding deliberated for days before he decided to buy a cat for his seven-year-old daughter. In March 1991 he had just reached the point where he could afford to move his family to a quiet suburb of Seattle, and he thought it would be nice if Kimberly had a pet.

But Harding had lost several cats when he was a boy. He would just begin to grow attached to them when they would either wander off and never return or would meet with fatal accidents on the street in front of their home in El Cajon, California. He had come to consider cats unstable, unreliable, perfidious creatures —that were also very accident prone.

When he brought home Elvira, a young black female, he had a little talk prepared to protect Kimberly's feelings. He told her that cats were more like visitors than permanent members of the family. Cats should be treated with love and respect, but one should never expect them to stay for very long. Kimberly should not be hurt or take it personally if Elvira just up and disappeared one day.

As the months went by and Elvira turned out to be a regular homebody and a wonderful friend to Kimberly, Harding began to wonder whether the jinx he had always experienced with cats had at last been broken.

"Elvira has brought Kimberly so much happiness," Karen Harding, Greg's wife, said to him one evening. "I'm so happy you were able to rise above your own childhood disappointment in cats."

On the night when Elvira failed to return home, Harding felt he might be guilty of some terrible self-fulfilling prophecy. He stood quietly at the door of Kimberly's bedroom as she asked in her evening prayers for Elvira please to come home to her.

Harding knew well the pain that his daughter felt, and a small voice in the back of his brain kept nagging, "I told you so. Cats never stay."

That night the temperature dropped, and although it seldom snowed heavily around Seattle, enough of the white stuff piled up on the ground to cause Kimberly additional concern for Elvira.

"Elvira will freeze to death, Daddy," she said, fighting back her tears the next afternoon when she came home from elementary school. "We have to go find her."

Harding knew locating a straying cat would be no small job in their area, which was still in the process of being transformed from farms and orchards to houses and yards. A number of rapidly deteriorating barns and outbuildings stood around the area. Elvira could be holed up in any of a hundred places—or she could have been killed by traffic, an unleashed dog, or one of the raccoons that stubbornly hung on to their rapidly vanishing turf.

"Please, Daddy, we have to go out and look for Elvira!"

Karen saw to it that they were both well bundled against the cold, and father and daughter set out in the gathering darkness in search of their missing cat.

In spite of Harding's growing pessimism, after about five minutes of Kimberly's plaintive calling, they seemed to hear answering meows from an old, falling-down barn.

Harding had to keep a firm grasp on his daughter's hand to stop her from running on ahead. He could not risk her stumbling over snow-covered debris or stepping on a rusty nail.

When the two of them finally found Elvira, it was hard to tell which of them was more amazed. The black cat had wrapped her furry self around the half-naked body of a very small baby girl.

"See Daddy," Kimberly said, smiling through her tears of joy. "Elvira wasn't being naughty by staying out all night. She was taking care of the baby!"

The doctors at a nearby clinic agreed that the deathly pale baby would surely have frozen without the cat's constant attention. The abandoned child, only a few months old, had been kept alive by Elvira's body heat and by her vigorous licking. Thanks to the cat's intervention, "Baby Doe" would recover without any complications.

"Elvira is a hero, isn't she, Daddy?" Kimberly asked on the way home from the clinic, as she hugged the purring cat close. "She couldn't come home if she was going to save the baby girl's life!"

Harding agreed that Elvira must be forgiven for staying out all night without checking in. "Elvira is a hero," he repeated.

—Brad Steiger

Hats Off to Ringo

We adopted Ringo, our red tabby, as a stray from a litter found outside my mother's nursing home. We had three cats and didn't want any more, but Ringo worked his way into our hearts. Had we stuck to our convictions, we would be dead today.

Last summer, we developed symptoms ranging from oversleeping to high blood pressure. Ray was recovering from heart surgery, and I had a full leg cast from an accident. We thought these symptoms were part of our illnesses. We were wrong!

On August 19, Ringo started slamming his body against the doors of our house. I let him out and he meowed loudly. He wanted me to follow him to the south side of our house, where we never go. Only our air-conditioner and gas and water meters are there.

Ringo dug near the gas meter, in jagged lava-rock landscaping. He lifted his head, opened his mouth, and wrinkled his nose to let me know something smelled awful. When I leaned over, the smell of natural gas bowled me over. I called the gas company immediately. We were at explosive levels around our foundation. A pilot light or a spark outdoors was all that stood between us and oblivion.

The gas had permeated the walls of our home and traveled up into our south bedroom. Our doctor said that if we hadn't had an explosion, we would have succumbed to methane poisoning. The plumbers found a steel coupler that had split open. The crack was growing larger due to rust and corrosion. Ringo had smelled the escaping gas four feet beneath our landscaping. What a nose for trouble!

Ringo shattered the myth that cats are indifferent. He led us to the gas leak that we couldn't smell and the meter couldn't register.

So, hats off to our dear Ringo. He is truly our hero!

—Carol and Ray Steiner

The Cat Who Saved Christmas

The old woman lived in a small house with her cane and her only companion, her mixed-breed kitten, Kitty. But that Christmas Eve was a joyful one as Eva Chesney bundled up against the cold Wisconsin winter. Moving slowly around her aging, century-old house, Eva fed small logs into her wood-burning furnace, looked out at the snowdrifts that reflected brilliant light into the night, and bid "Merry Christmas!" to Kitty.

The next morning would bring a white Christmas to Stevens Point—and Kitty's first Christmas with Eva. Eva, seventy, had recently adopted the kitten; and even though Kitty was only a few months old, Eva was thrilled to have companionship. It was so much less lonely with Kitty to care for.

As midnight approached, Eva took her cane and slowly made her way up the narrow staircase. Eva was weary but Kitty still wiggled with energy, weaving playfully in and out of her master's feet as she headed down the hallway to bed. At the threshold, Eva bid Kitty good night and gently shut the door. The master of the house couldn't sleep with a kitten pouncing all night!

When she, too, grew tired, Kitty went downstairs and curled up on the rug near the warmth of the furnace.

When Kitty awoke it was about 4:30 in the morning, the furnace was still blazing, and the kitten was already weak from deadly carbon-monoxide poisoning. The furnace had overheated, sending gray-black smoke pouring out of the chimney into a basement laundry chute. Dense, oxygen-eating smoke was already rolling through all the downstairs rooms and pluming upstairs.

Struggling to stand, Kitty could have headed toward the fresh chill seeping under the front door. Or tried to leap onto the first-floor windowsills to paw at the glass separating her from the cool night air.

Instead, she crawled slowly, under blooming black smoke clouds, deeper into the burning house, toward the dense smoke where even her superior night vision was powerless—toward the stairs. At the base of the staircase, gasping for breath, the little kitten reached her paws up on the first riser. The stairs she gleefully romped up and down all day loomed ahead of her like a chain of mountains. Gasping for breath, her little paws slipping weakly on the treads, she made her climb toward her master's room.

The kitten meowed weakly in the hallway, but there was no sound inside Eva's room. Kitty began to claw at the door with what little strength she had left.

In moments there was noise behind the door. Alerted by Kitty, Eva awoke, smelled the burning, and fumbled for her cane in the dark. Eva gasped as she opened the bedroom door and was blasted by foul black smoke, but she kept her balance. The weak kitty meows were like a beacon guiding her down the hall to the stairs. Kitty, now barely able to crawl, slid downward, following the familiar thump of Eva's cane on the stairs.

In moments Eva lurched outside, gasping the cool night air. But Kitty couldn't follow. Overcome by fumes, she collapsed on the last step. As dawn broke and Stevens Point began to celebrate Christmas, Eva was alive and unharmed and began to tell the story of her heroic little Kitty—a story that captured headlines and hearts around the country. Kitty, it was said, had given the greatest Christmas gift of all—sacrificing her own life to save someone she loved.

—*From* **Real Animal Heroes**
by Paul Drew Stevens
(Adapted by Michael Capuzzo)

Blacky to the Rescue

In the spring of 1987, my wife and I moved to the country, six miles from town. We loved the peaceful setting, but it was heartbreaking to see so many abandoned cats. We trapped several strays, had them neutered or spayed by a vet, and found homes for them.

One day a very large black cat—solid muscle, scary looking with many scars and the wild look of a homeless animal—strolled onto our property, warily keeping his distance. The big tom followed my wife everywhere she went. Cleaning the barns, feeding the horses—he was there, watching from a distance. We couldn't trap him, he was too smart. It turned out we didn't need to. After carefully watching us for a while, Blacky decided to adopt us.

One day, some folks down the road from us who raised cats for money were evicted from their house and left the cats behind in cages. I heard the animal control officer and a neighbor discussing the problem —the officer said he had no authority to trespass and retrieve the cats in the cages. "Don't worry," my neighbor said, "the cats will be gone tomorrow." Little did I know my neighbor planned to dispose of them.

I never heard the gunshots. But the next day when I came home from lunch I heard a small mewing noise in the garage and went to look—there was Blacky, lying next to a tiny gray-and-white male kitten who'd been shot with a small-caliber gun. Blacky, with the help of our vet, saved the kitten's life, and nursed him lovingly back to health. We kept the kitten and called him Boo.

While Blacky and Boo played together like father and son, our two female cats, Prissy and Delila, were always fighting. One day I mentioned to my wife we should get a female kitten to break up the friction. Two days later, I heard a kitten meowing in the garage. I looked under our truck and to my amazement I saw a baby female kitten, barely weaned. Blacky was lying proudly beside her, grooming and caring for "Ty" just as he did for Boo. Prissy eventually died of cancer, but her last days were happier ones as Blacky's little kitten kept her so busy she forgot all about her arguments with Delila. Once again it was Blacky, our country tom, to the rescue.

—*Douglas Burford*

Shade McCorkle

There is a story of a tiny southern woman of a certain age and a big gray cat of uncertain parentage whose deeds will be remembered as long as records are kept. I tell it to anyone who seems cynical about cats and their courage and devotion to human beings. It's a true story: Memphis, Tennessee, December 1932.

It was the year William Faulkner wrote *Light in August*. Amelia Earhart became the first woman to fly solo across the Atlantic. Franklin Delano Roosevelt beat Herbert Hoover, blamed by voters for the Depression, in a landslide.

Nell Mitchell, a frail, sickly, eighty-eight-pound

woman, was asleep, alone in her house with her cat, a dark, gray-striped mix named Shade McCorkle.

Nell's housekeeper had already tidied up and left. Before leaving, she summoned Dr. Longset to come care for Nell, whose condition was worsening. The doctor had arrived, given Nell an injection of medication, and expressed concern that she would be alone for the evening. Don't worry, Nell assured him, her husband soon would be home.

After the doctor left, Nell drifted in and out of a fitful sleep on the daybed. Shade McCorkle nestled into the gray afghan tucked across his mistress's feet.

Sometime later, there was a knock on the porch door. Shifting groggily on the daybed, Nell didn't get up, Shade slumbered on under the afghan. Nell knew it wasn't her husband—he would have used the key and called out a greeting. Too ill and fatigued to rise, Nell prayed the visitor would simply go away.

Instead, she heard the screen door of the porch swing open. The sound of footsteps, this time inside the house. Someone was walking toward the kitchen. Nell lay still, her heart racing, helpless. She was startled when the kitchen's inner door flew open.

A thin, grubby-looking young man was in the room, his eyes wandering everywhere and finally settling on the old woman, so tiny there was hardly any shape at all under the blanket.

Angrily, he demanded something to eat.

"Go next door," Nell implored. "I'm too ill."

The intruder grabbed a chair and pulled it to the old woman's side. He settled into it, grinning, with a menacing air.

"Who was the tall guy who just left?" he demanded.

Nell was so groggy she almost couldn't speak. Fear forced the words out. "Dr. Longset," Nell said, the words slurred from the medicine.

"When will your old man be back?"

The old woman was confused and afraid. Where was her husband? She had lost all concept of time. She could feel Shade slumbering, lying beneath the covers.

Suddenly, the intruder demanded Nell's ring. Frightened, she pulled the ring from her bony, veined finger. She prayed that he would simply rob her—that he wouldn't hurt her.

Without warning the man jerked her up by the collar, wrenching her neck and torso from the daybed, and slapped her across the face with an open hand. The pain was terrible. Terrified, Nell braced herself for another blow. The man glowered over her, threatening— but he never had a chance.

Fourteen pounds of fury exploded from beneath the afghan. Shade McCorkle sprang to the man's shoulders, grabbed his throat with his claws and ripped with his fangs. Yowling in terror, the man spun around the room, grabbing for the cat, punching at air, spurting blood, knocking over furniture, wheeling blindly.

"Call him off!" the man screamed at Nell. Shade held on, tearing chunks of skin from the man's face and neck. The man grabbed Shade's throat, trying to strangle him, ripped the cat off and threw him with tremendous force across the room. He took the cat and slammed him down viciously against a table.

But in a flash Shade leaped back, clawing onto the man's face and renewing his ferocious attack. The last thing Nell heard before she fainted was the man screaming and running away down the street.

Nell Mitchell survived her attacker, and was able to tell the world of her pet's heroics. Shade McCorkle was badly beaten and bruised, but recovered to win the Latham Foundation's Gold Medal for animal heroism. The Latham Foundation stopped recognizing animal heroism almost forty years ago, but you can still look it up. It was 1932, the year the Thoroughbred Burgoo King won the Kentucky Derby and another animal, a mixed-breed of only fourteen pounds, became an American classic.

—*From* **Real Animal Heroes**
by Paul Drew Stevens
(Adapted by Michael Capuzzo)

Phantom to the Rescue

Shortly after my father died, four years ago, my friend gave me Phantom, my cat. Phantom was just a kitten then, and it was a time of need for both of us. Phantom had been adopted from the humane society, but my friend was allergic and couldn't keep him.

I took him on a trial basis, as I had never had a pet before. I didn't even know how to hold a kitten. There was an adjustment period (of one day) before I fell in love with my best friend. He helped me through my loss and is always there for me.

On January 19, 1996, during our worst blizzard in a decade in southern New Jersey, I was asleep when a fire began in my bedroom. An electric fire was behind the wall, smoking and sparking—a fire that threatened the entire complex I live in. It was five in the morning, and I was sleeping right through it. Suddenly, Phantom jumped on my head, meowing so loud that I woke up. I was barely conscious, but I smelled smoke and heard sparks. Fumbling nervously, I called 911. Within six minutes firemen were there to put out the fire, saving my life and many others'.

A week later, January 25 was declared Phantom the Cat Day in New Jersey by U.S. Congressional Proclamation. I will be forever grateful to my best friend, my beautiful, green-eyed, gray Phantom. Already, he has saved me twice.

—*Judi Smoller*

Booshita to the Rescue

I believe things happen for good if you strongly believe they will.

One day, twenty years ago, I visited a neighbor who had two kittens, strays her grandsons had brought home not knowing how to love and care for them. Both kittens jumped to my lap, and immediately I knew they felt the security they needed. When I was ready to leave they followed me in a way that made me understand they were asking for help. My neighbor told me: "If you want them, they are yours. I am going to get rid of both anyway."

I gave them love and care as I always do with animals. We celebrated their eighth birthday with the children in our new neighborhood. Eventually, one of the cats had an accident and died at thirteen years old. It was really sad. We mourned him for a long time.

We took good care of the female, Booshita. She was special to me, slept with me, and followed me all the time. When she was sick she ate from my hands—baby food with a baby's spoon. Life went on and I always had the feeling that cat was God's instrument for the sake of our family.

One day, after my husband left for work, I was alone with Booshita in the family room watching TV. Suddenly, I remembered I had not locked one of the rear doors, so I got up to check. Booshita ran ahead of me and got in my way, blocking my path so I could not move. I saw she was nervous, excited, the hairs on her tail and spine were raised, and she was making strange growling noises. Because of Booshita, I was alarmed and scared, and I moved quickly. Then I looked through the glass door and saw a man trying to break in. He had one of the unlocked doors already halfway open. I ran to the burglar alarm panic button and activated the alarm at the same time screaming like mad. Hearing this, the man ran away. Later, I learned that same man tried to kill a woman two blocks away. I think there is nothing left to say. I understood Booshita.

Years later we had gone shopping for a short time, when I felt Booshita was waiting for me back home. When I took her in my arms, I know she felt her days were over, and I could feel she sensed the same security as she did years before when she was a little kitten. She died in my arms after twenty years of mutual happiness. We buried Booshita in May in a special coffin that my husband made for her. I miss her so, my wise old Booshita, my companion, protector, and soul mate,

who taught me animals communicate with us in ways
we don't yet understand.

—*Carmen J. Garcés*

Andora

As an insulin-dependent diabetic, I have insulin reactions occasionally. During such times, my family would
become aware of the problem and knew what to do:
either orange juice or a trip to the emergency room.

Once my children were grown and out of the house
and my husband worked nights, I would eat a little
extra at night to prevent insulin reactions. But diabetes
has a mind of its own. One night I was sleeping when,
unknown to me, I started having an insulin reaction
that, unchecked, could have left me in an irreversible
coma or caused my death. My cat, Andora, started slap-
ping my face with her paws, claws retracted, and nudging me with her head until I was awake enough to
realize what was happening. I knew I had to get something to eat before going back to sleep. My beautiful
cat saved my life this way several times. She died last
year after eighteen years of being a loving, gentle pet. I
miss her so.

—*Margo Meyer*

Priscilla

When we adopted our cat Priscilla from the humane society she was ten months old with grape green eyes and soft gray fur. Priscilla was the smartest cat I ever saw. If we couldn't find her in the apartment she'd be perched on the top of an open door looking at us looking for her. Once she ran out the front door, up the hallway stairs, into an open apartment where three men were playing cards, and ran between their legs; I ran after her, retrieving her from under the table. The three men kept playing cards as if nothing had happened.

One day, she stood facing the door to our apartment meowing plaintively for hours on end, day and night, for two days. My wife and I kept looking out the door, but saw nothing unusual. Finally we thought to knock on the door of our elderly neighbor's apartment across the hall from us. There was no answer. We got the manager and he unlocked the door for us. The old woman was in her bathtub with a broken hip, unable to move. She'd been in that tub for two days. She was taken to the hospital and released after treatment. Priscilla, happy to help, returned to her perch atop the open door, looking down on all of us.

—*Harry and Jeanne Bergman*

Pussy Willow Saves the Day

Once my cat, Pussy Willow, went to get his usual mouse dinner. While he was out, our neighbor's dog got loose and ripped the cage front off of our rabbits' hutch. Our two rabbits ran into the woods. They were gone for three hours, and we thought they were gone forever. I was crying very hard. But when our cat got home, he had found one of the rabbits! We saw his face when he returned with the rabbit. His face clearly expressed what he thought. He thought, "Hey guys, you lost something." The rabbit was hopping alongside Pussy Willow, with Pussy Willow nudging him with his nose back to our house. I went to Pussy Willow and said, "Thank you so much!" Then we petted Pussy Willow till his fur went staticky. He is our hero!

—*Lisa Dannen, age 8*

CHAPTER EIGHT

Healing and Faith

There are two means of refuge from the miseries of life: Music and Cats.

Albert Schweitzer

In Memoriam Leo: A Yellow Cat,
Whisper some kindly word, to bless
A wistful soul who understands
That life is but one long caress
Of gentle words and gentle hands.

Margaret Sherwood

The Butcher's Kitten

I was a preschooler in 1938; and although the worst of the Depression was behind us, our family still struggled to subsist. My mother didn't go to the butcher as frequently as she'd have liked, so it was a real treat for me when I was taken along. I was fascinated by the sights and smells of the butcher's shop.

One day, as mother waited her turn, the butcher's wife came over to me, silently took my hand, and with her finger to her lips, motioned me to be silent. She winked as if she had an incredible treat in store, and I slipped along, trustingly, into a rear room where I beheld a wondrous, fat mamma cat feeding her litter of beautiful kittens.

"Which do you think is the prettiest?" she queried. Without hesitating I pointed to one, although in retrospect I think they may have all been identical. The kitty I selected was then placed in a brown bag and I was instructed to grip each side without crushing the "contents" and to be certain to leave some air space for breathing. Her final words were, "Don't say anything to your mother until you get home. She'll be so surprised!"

Mom stared at me as I emerged with a jiggling bag tightly clasped as ordered. She gave a knowing look to the butcher's wife, and we soon left.

On the way home, my mother asked me what I was carrying, but faithful to my promise I didn't reveal a thing. Soon, however, the bag began to tear and my secret was literally "out." I carried my darling close to my face with care, while softly breathing loving endearments and gently caressing my new best friend.

Each day thereafter, I was given ten cents to return to the butcher for some lung to feed the cat. My brothers protested that *we* didn't eat meat every day, but what else would one feed a cat? Other than her daily ration of milk, we had no idea.

My brothers decided to name her Mouser after rejecting my suggestion of Cinderella and so Mouser became a member of our family, even living up to her name. One Thanksgiving she bumped the outside of our dining room window with a big, wiggling rat held tightly in her mouth—her contribution to our Thanksgiving feast!

Another holiday, while my mother was concentrating on preparing a plump chicken for soup, Mouser stealthfully grabbed a chicken quarter with her sharp teeth and ran out of the kitchen. Not to be outwitted, my mother followed her, flying up two flights of stairs, and cornered her against a closed bedroom door.

My father and I were convulsed with laughter at the sight of my mother screaming, "You rotten thief!" as she and Mouser engaged in a tug-of-war for the chicken breast. (Although losing a fresh fat chicken quarter to a wily cat was no laughing matter in those lean days.) That night at dinner, my mother complained, "Imagine having a robber in the family."

Mouser soon became my amusing pet and my nemesis, creating all sorts of mischief for which my brothers blamed me. But I did not love her any the less. We played, and snuggled, and loved.

When I was almost seven, I developed a ruptured appendix and became gravely ill. I was hospitalized for weeks, lingering between life and death, before recovery was ensured.

When I returned home, a strange phenomenon occurred. Mouser paced back and forth beside my bed for what seemed like endless hours, interrupting her routine only when the doorbell rang. She then ran and approached the caller, bumping her body against our guest's leg repeatedly, while calling out in a mournful wail, demanding, as it were, that she be followed to my room.

This happened again and again. Mouser would knock her body against the legs of callers; first one leg, then the other, emitting her eerie wails, until the caller understood clearly that Mouser was to be followed.

Once the visitor was in my bedroom, Mouser engaged in her pacing routine—keeping herself between my bed and my visitor. My parents talked about this for months, amazed that our cat had sensed the gravity of my illness and was now protecting me, while alerting outsiders that I was at last recovering at home.

Mouser died after the war; years later the butcher shop closed, a little girl grew up, and the cherished family life she knew changed, over time, forever. But the lessons of Mouser always stayed with me. My cat had demonstrated to me the meaning of loyalty and served as an example of a treasured value: love between species. I have learned to care about the ill, the grieving, and the needy; and my heart goes out to comfort those in the healing process. My perception of compassionate humanity was deepened by my faithful, guileless teacher, my cat Mouser. I miss him so!

—*Bettyanne Gray*

The Persian Cat

EDITORS' NOTE: Until our current modern love
affair with cats—and by current we mean the past
twenty years, when the number of cats in American
households doubled and stories of love and devotion
slowly emerged—the cat was portrayed harshly in
Western literature. He was mysterious, cunning, le-
thal, and smug.

Typical was a story told in Germany, "The Pot of
Fat," in which a cat professes love and affection for a
mouse and persuades the mouse to move in with him
and share a pot of fat to keep them through the winter. In short order, the cat devours both the pot of fat
and the mouse. "And that is the way of the world,"
the story concludes.

Malachi McCormick has traced a tradition of
such cat stories, stories marked by "realpolitik and
cynicism and the big lie," to the so-called civilized or
industrially developed countries of the West.

Cat stories have not always been so cynical. This is
a story told for many centuries. Handed down orally
from generation to generation, its sources of author-
ship are unclear. Its original source, however, is as
clear and eternal as the springs of the heart.

Long before cynicism became the way of the world,
a merchant of Isfahan, the fabled city of Persia, came
upon a group of thieves in the act of beating and robbing a stranger.

Without thought for his own safety, the merchant
dispersed the ruffians into the desert, then turned to
help the unfortunate stranger, paying for lodging and
food at a local caravansary and insisting on staying by
his side until he recovered.

The next evening, the stranger was sufficiently restored to be able to sit with the merchant by a fire outside the tent. High above the dark green palm trees, the stars shone bright and crisp in the midnight blue of the sky. The smoke from the fire coiled gently upward in a cooling breeze, forming and reforming itself into an endless procession of shifting shapes.

After a long silence in which they both gazed into the fire, the stranger touched the merchant on the sleeve and said: "My friend, you knew nothing about me, but you did not hesitate to come to my rescue, with no expectation of recompense, which is a true mark of a great soul.

"But now I wish to give you a gift in return. You did not know that I am a magician, and can give you anything in the world that you desire."

The merchant replied: "I have lived a very good and happy life with my family. I have been successful in my trading and right now could desire nothing more than to sit here in this beautiful and peaceful place, watching the fire, the swirling smoke, and the stars."

The magician nodded. "Very well. I shall therefore make for you a gift out of those very materials, so you shall have it forever."

And he took a little tongue of fire, and the light of two distant stars, and a skein of swirling gray smoke, and kneaded and formed it in the basket of his deftly moving hands. And there came from within a sweet mewing sound and a rich purr, and out crept the most wonderful little cat that ever had been seen, with thick short gray fur, bright eyes, and fire-tipped tongue. And it played and purred and waved its tail like the swirling smoke.

The magician bade the merchant: "Take this great soul back to your home, and it will be a friend to your family and a thing of beauty in your household for the rest of your days."

And that is the strange and wonderful story of how the Persian cat came into this world.

—*Folktale retold by Malachi McCormick*

A Gift from Licorice

He came to us through a Free-to-Good-Home ad on our supermarket's bulletin board. We had just moved into our new town house and decided a cat would be the perfect pet. The ad said he was a declawed, neutered kitten. When we called and went to see him we discovered he was no kitten, but the most beautiful black cat! We decided then and there to bring him home with us.

He adjusted quite well, but for some unknown reason, didn't cotton to me right away, even though I fed him, cleaned his litter box, and loved him the best I could. One day when I was in my bedroom, he followed me and suddenly he grabbed my leg and gave it quite a scratch. My husband was furious and told him if he did that again, out he would go. From that day on, he never bit or scratched me. He really seemed to be my husband's cat, but tolerated me, even though I was the one who really wanted him.

A year and a half later, my husband passed away, and Licorice was there to feel and hear my grief. The week after the funeral, when I returned home from staying with my daughter, I went to bed alone in my own house for the first time. As I lay in bed trying to sleep, my heart was heavy with feelings of grief and loss, and it was a relief to hear Licorice somewhere in the dark talking the way he does when he carries his favorite toy, a gray mouse. I fell asleep thinking Licorice was going to play since he always liked to play late at night.

When I awoke the next morning, the gray mouse was right next to me on my husband's side of the bed.

Licorice, being the smart cat he was, didn't want me to be lonely. He was such a good cat and a joy to have around. Three years ago, very suddenly, he developed feline leukemia and died a week later. I had to make the decision to put him to sleep and to this day miss him terribly.

I am not alone, as Lizzie has sneaked into my heart; but she knows she will never replace Licorice, and she is happy with that. That first night alone after my husband died Licorice had brought me a gift I will never forget, and showed me how much he cared.

—*Martha P. Beatty*

The Christmas Kitten

My strongest memory of Christmas will always be bound up with a certain little cat.

I first saw her when I was called to see one of Mrs. Ainsworth's dogs, and I looked in some surprise at the furry black creature sitting before the fire.

"I didn't know you had a cat," I said.

The lady smiled. "We haven't, this is Debbie."

"Debbie?"

"Yes, at least that's what we call her. She's a stray. Comes here two or three times a week and we give her some food. I don't know where she lives but I believe she spends a lot of her time around one of the farms along the road."

"Do you ever get the feeling she wants to stay with you?"

"No." Mrs. Ainsworth shook her head. "She's a timid little thing. Just creeps in, has some food then flits away. There's something so appealing about her but she doesn't seem to want to let me or anybody into her life."

I looked again at the little cat. "But she isn't just having food today."

"That's right. It's a funny thing but every now and again she slips through here into the lounge and sits by the fire for a few minutes. It's as though she was giving herself a treat."

"Yes . . . I see what you mean." There was no doubt there was something unusual in the attitude of the little animal. She was sitting bolt upright on the thick rug which lay before the fireplace in which the coals glowed and flamed. She made no effort to curl up or wash herself or do anything other than gaze quietly ahead. And there was something in the dusty black of her coat, the half-wild scrawny look of her, that gave

me a clue. This was a special event in her life, a rare
and wonderful thing; she was lapping up a comfort un-
dreamed of in her daily existence.

As I watched she turned, crept soundlessly from the
room and was gone.

"That's always the way with Debbie," Mrs. Ainsworth laughed. "She never stays more than ten minutes
or so, then she's off."

She was a plumpish, pleasant-faced woman in her
forties and the kind of client veterinary surgeons dream
of; well off, generous, and the owner of three cosseted
basset hounds. And it only needed the habitually
mournful expressions of one of the dogs to deepen a
little, and I was round there posthaste. Today one of
the bassets had raised its paw and scratched its ear a
couple of times and that was enough to send its mistress scurrying to the phone in great alarm.

So my visits to the Ainsworth home were frequent
but undemanding, and I had ample opportunity to look
out for the little cat that had intrigued me. On one
occasion I spotted her nibbling daintily from a saucer
at the kitchen door. As I watched she turned and almost floated on light footsteps into the hall, then
through the lounge door.

The three bassets were already in residence, draped
snoring on the fireside rug, but they seemed to be used
to Debbie because two of them sniffed her in a bored
manner and the third merely cocked a sleepy eye at her
before flopping back on the rich pile.

Debbie sat among them in her usual posture; upright, intent, gazing absorbedly into the glowing coals.
This time I tried to make friends with her. I approached her carefully but she leaned away as I
stretched out my hand. However, by patient wheedling
and soft talk I managed to touch her and gently stroke
her cheek with one finger. There was a moment when

she responded by putting her head on one side and rubbing back against my hand but soon she was ready to leave. Once outside the house she darted quickly along the road, then through a gap in a hedge, and the last I saw was the little black figure flitting over the rain-swept grass of a field.

"I wonder where she goes," I murmured half to myself.

Mrs. Ainsworth appeared at my elbow. "That's something we've never been able to find out."

It must have been nearly three months before I heard from Mrs. Ainsworth, and in fact I had begun to wonder at the basset's long symptomless run when she came on the phone.

It was Christmas morning, and she was apologetic. "Mr. Herriot, I'm so sorry to bother you today of all days. I should think you want a rest at Christmas like anybody else." But her natural politeness could not hide the distress in her voice.

"Please don't worry about that," I said. "Which one is it this time?"

"It's not one of the dogs. It's . . . Debbie."

"Debbie? She's at your house now?"

"Yes . . . but there's something wrong. Please come quickly."

Driving through the marketplace I thought again that Darrowby on Christmas Day was like Dickens come to life; the empty square with the snow thick on the cobbles and hanging from the eaves of the fretted lines of roofs; the shops closed and the coloured lights of the Christmas trees winking at the windows of the clustering houses, warmly inviting against the cold white bulk of the fells behind.

Mrs. Ainsworth's home was lavishly decorated with tinsel and holly, rows of drinks stood on the sideboard and the rich aroma of turkey and sage and onion stuffing wafted from the kitchen. But her eyes were full of pain as she led me through to the lounge.

Debbie was there all right, but this time everything was different. She wasn't sitting upright in her usual position; she was stretched quite motionless on her side, and huddled close to her lay a tiny black kitten.

I looked down in bewilderment. "What's happened here?"

"It's the strangest thing," Mrs. Ainsworth replied. "I haven't seen her for several weeks, then she came in about two hours ago—sort of staggered into the kitchen, and she was carrying the kitten in her mouth. She took it through to the lounge and laid it on the rug and at first I was amused. But I could see all was not well because she sat as she usually does, but for a long time—over an hour—then she lay down like this and she hasn't moved."

I knelt on the rug and passed my hand over Debbie's neck and ribs. She was thinner than ever, her fur dirty and mud caked. She did not resist as I gently opened her mouth. The tongue and mucous membranes were abnormally pale and the lips ice cold against my fingers. When I pulled down her eyelid and saw the dead white conjunctiva a knell sounded in my mind.

I palpated the abdomen with a grim certainty as to what I would find and there was no surprise, only a dull sadness as my fingers closed around a hard lobulated mass deep among the viscera. Massive lymphosarcoma. Terminal and hopeless. I put my stethoscope on her heart and listened to the increasingly faint, rapid beat, then I straightened up and sat on the rug looking sightlessly into the fireplace, feeling the warmth of the flames on my face.

Mrs. Ainsworth's voice seemed to come from afar. "Is she ill, Mr. Herriot?"

I hesitated. "Yes . . . yes, I'm afraid so. She has a malignant growth." I stood up. "There's absolutely nothing I can do. I'm sorry."

"Oh!" Her hand went to her mouth and she looked at me wide-eyed. When at last she spoke her voice trembled. "Well, you must put her to sleep immediately. It's the only thing to do. We can't let her suffer."

"Mrs. Ainsworth," I said. "There's no need. She's dying now—in a coma—far beyond suffering."

She turned quickly away from me and was very still as she fought with her emotions. Then she gave up the struggle and dropped on her knees beside Debbie.

"Oh, poor little thing!" she sobbed, and stroked the cat's head again and again as the tears fell unchecked on the matted fur. "What she must have come through. I feel I ought to have done more for her."

For a few moments I was silent, feeling her sorrow, so discordant among the bright seasonal colours of this festive room. Then I spoke gently.

"Nobody could have done more than you," I said. "Nobody could have been kinder."

"But I'd have kept her here—in comfort. It must have been terrible out there in the cold when she was so desperately ill—I daren't think about it. And having kittens, too—I . . . I wonder how many she did have?"

I shrugged. "I don't suppose we'll ever know. Maybe just this one. It happens sometimes. And she brought it to you, didn't she?"

"Yes . . . that's right . . . she did . . . she did." Mrs. Ainsworth reached out and lifted the bedraggled black morsel. She smoothed her finger along the muddy fur and the tiny mouth opened in a soundless *miaow.* "Isn't it strange? She was dying, and she brought her kitten here. And on Christmas Day."

I bent and put my hand on Debbie's heart. There was no beat.

I looked up. "I'm afraid she's gone." I lifted the small body, almost feather light, wrapped it in the sheet that had been spread on the rug and took it out to the car.

When I came back Mrs. Ainsworth was still stroking the kitten. The tears had dried on her cheeks and she was bright-eyed as she looked at me.

"I've never had a cat before," she said.

I smiled. "Well, it looks as though you've got one now."

And she certainly had. That kitten grew rapidly into a sleek handsome cat with a boisterous nature, which earned him the name of Buster. In every way he was the opposite of his timid little mother. Not for him the privations of the secret outdoor life; he stalked the rich carpets of the Ainsworth home like a king, and the ornate collar he always wore added something more to his presence.

On my visits I watched his development with delight, but the occasion that stays in my mind was the following Christmas Day, a year from his arrival.

I was out on my rounds as usual. I can't remember when I haven't had to work on Christmas Day because the animals have never got round to recognising it as a holiday; but with the passage of the years the vague resentment I used to feel has been replaced by philosophical acceptance. After all, as I tramped around the hillside barns in the frosty air, I was working up a better appetite for my turkey than all the millions lying in bed or slumped by the fire; and this was aided by the innumerable aperitifs I received from the hospitable farmers.

I was on my way home, bathed in a rosy glow. I had consumed several whiskies—the kind the inexpert Yorkshiremen pour as though it were ginger ale—and I had finished with a glass of old Mrs. Earnshaw's rhubarb wine, which has seared its way straight to my toenails. I heard the cry as I was passing Mrs. Ainsworth's house.

"Merry Christmas, Mr. Herriot!" She was letting a visitor out of the front door, and she waved at me gaily. "Come in and have a drink to warm you up."

I didn't need warming up but I pulled in at the kerb without hesitation. In the house there was all the festive cheer of last year and the same glorious whiff of sage and onion, which set my gastric juices surging. But there was not the sorrow; there was Buster.

He was darting up to each of the dogs in turn, ears pricked, eyes blazing with devilment, dabbing a paw at them then streaking away.

Mrs. Ainsworth laughed. "You know, he plagues the life out of them. Gives them no peace."

She was right. To the bassets, Buster's arrival was rather like the intrusion of an irreverent outsider into an exclusive London club. For a long time they had led a life of measured grace; regular sedate walks with their mistress, superb food in ample quantities, and long snoring sessions on the rugs and armchairs. Their days followed one upon another in unruffled calm. And then came Buster.

He was dancing up to the youngest dog again, sideways this time, head on one side, goading him. When he started boxing with both paws it was too much even for the basset. He dropped his dignity and rolled over with the cat in a brief wrestling match.

"I want to show you something." Mrs. Ainsworth

lifted a hard rubber ball from the sideboard and went out to the garden, followed by Buster. She threw the ball across the lawn and the cat bounded after it over the frosted grass, the muscles rippling under the black sheen of his coat. He seized the ball in his teeth, brought it back to his mistress, dropped it at her feet and waited expectantly. She threw it and he brought it back again.

I gasped incredulously. A feline retriever!

The bassets looked on disdainfully. Nothing would ever have induced them to chase a ball, but Buster did it again and again as though he would never tire of it.

Mrs. Ainsworth turned to me. "Have you ever seen anything like that?"

"No," I replied. "I never have. He is a most remarkable cat."

She snatched Buster from his play and we went back into the house, where she held him close to her face, laughing as the big cat purred and arched himself ecstatically against her cheek.

Looking at him, a picture of health and contentment, my mind went back to his mother. Was it too much to think that that dying little creature with the last of her strength had carried her kitten to the only haven of comfort and warmth she had ever known in the hope that it would be cared for there? Maybe it was.

But it seemed I wasn't the only one with such fancies. Mrs. Ainsworth turned to me and though she was smiling her eyes were wistful.

"Debbie would be pleased," she said.

I nodded. "Yes, she would. . . . It was just a year ago today she brought him, wasn't it?"

"That's right." She hugged Buster to her again. "The best Christmas present I ever had."

—*James Herriot*

The Purpose

The ability of dogs to love and heal is well known, but cats, too, possess this special power. In 1989, my son Steven was very ill. He and his brother, Michael, both suffered from cystic fibrosis. At the time, Steven had a very severe case of pneumonia. His brother had a pet cat named Katie. Steven had always wanted a cat of his own, but he was more specific. He wanted a black angora.

Steven was more frightened during this hospital stay than he had ever been, and I was desperate to do *something* to help him feel better. One day, I happened to notice in the classified ads an ad for free kittens. They were all different types, the ad said. The one that caught my eye was a black fluffy kitten. My husband and I hurried out to the address in the paper, hoping the black kitten was not gone. We were in luck! The kitten was so small it could fit in the palm of my hand and had the sweetest disposition. We examined the kitten and were sure it was a female so we took her.

Pets were not allowed in our local hospital, but Steven's spirits were so low that we decided to sneak the kitten in to help perk him up. The kitten fit easily into my pocket so it was easy to sneak her in. But we were like two kids playing spy—we giggled so much I was sure we'd be caught.

When we entered Steven's room, our son was so relieved to see us. It was the first time he had been alone since he entered the hospital. I told him we had a surprise for him and pulled the tiny kitten out of my pocket. The look of wonder and surprise on his face was worth everything to me.

After that, Steven's health began to improve. The kitten never left our son's side. When hospital personnel and doctors came in we were terrified that they would say something. But they never did. It was as if the kitten knew, because she always remained perfectly still while strangers were in the room.

One day after about a week, the doctor was examining Steven and the cat sneezed. The doctor jumped. He said, "I thought it was a stuffed animal." He was so pleased with Steven's improved health that he went to the hospital board and got the rules changed to allow pets to stay with their owners so long as they had all of their shots.

Steven named the kitten Marie. One day, while playing with Marie, he noticed that testicles had dropped into place. Since we didn't want to confuse the cat too much we changed Marie to Murry.

Murry was a great comfort to Steven. He seemed to sense when Steven was low and would rub his nose on Steven's face to be kissed. It always brought a smile to Steven.

On April 8, 1990, Steven died after a week of living on a ventilator. We were all devastated, especially Michael, his brother. We noticed that Murry kept searching the house for Steven and crying. Murry became even more special to me because Steven had loved him so much.

Two months after Steven's death, we moved to California. It was a long drive from Colorado, but Murry and Katie were calm travelers. In Needles, California, my husband rolled his window down four inches to get some air and without warning Murry hurtled himself out the window. He was so fast none of us could react. We saw, instantly, our beloved kitty killed by a tractor-trailer. It was nighttime in the desert and we were all stunned, then crying. We were devastated, doubly so as Murry was Steven's cat. But as the miles stretched ahead of us, it seemed as if Murry had come for a purpose and that purpose was over. It was almost as if he had given his life to be with Steven again.

—*Debra Matthew*

Felix the Cat

For many days and nights, my good friend Carol had been caring for her dog, Aspen, who was recovering from a difficult surgery. I offered to give her a rest for a while and care for Aspen at our farm. Aspen died while he was with me. I found him curled peacefully under an old shrub.

I knew that it was time for him to go, and that it was his choice; but I felt terrible that he died in my care. It was a really emotional time for me, and I was outside by the shrub crying hard for a long time.

I thought I'd done something wrong, or somehow hadn't seen the signs. Finally I went back into the house where my husband Jeff was holding our new cat, Felix.

I was telling Jeff how bad I felt about Aspen, and he went to hand me Felix for some comfort, but Felix didn't go from Jeff's arms to mine. Instead, he reached out and placed his paw on my heart, and he just left it there.

Suddenly, I felt this incredible energy and calmness

coming through that little paw. It was amazing. I looked at Jeff, and he looked at me and we both knew exactly what was taking place—Felix was just radiating love. He stayed like that for almost a full minute, and Jeff and I sat there bathed in the light of that incredible, timeless moment.

—Judee Curcio-Wolfe

The Angel Cat

During the first months following my cancer diagnosis, I wouldn't acknowledge any kind of healing but physical healing. I wasn't interested in techniques that could help me cope better or extend my life expectancy by a few months; mere remission or quality of life didn't capture my attention either. Full recovery was the only option I would accept, and I was willing to do anything, go anywhere, to achieve it.

When my surgeries and radiation treatments were over, I found myself in that frightening twilight zone of life after treatment. The doctors had done all they could, and I was on my own to wonder if I'd be alive or dead by the following year.

For the sake of my sanity, I tried hard to convince myself and anyone else who would listen that I was doing just fine and that cancer was no death sentence.

My motto became, "I don't write off cancer patients." I was ferocious and flailing.

Only two weeks earlier, my lover and I had parted ways. I was feeling confused and frightened about the future. Alone in bed at night, I would look at the white walls and wonder who would want a thirty-nine-year-old cancer patient. Life in my apartment was dismally quiet.

Then, Flora entered my life—a skinny feral kitten about four weeks old, full of ringworm, fleas, and earmites. Shivering and alone under the wheel well of my parked car, Flora looked desperately sick. I grabbed hold of her scraggly tail and tugged. Within seconds my hand was scratched to shreds, but I hung on and brought her, hissing and complaining, to my apartment. At that point, I realized that my lonely life welcomed the commotion of a tiny, angry kitten who would distract me from my own depressing thoughts.

With the arrival of the kitten, I pulled my energy away from myself and my fretful imaginings and concentrated on healing Flora. Along with ringworms and fleas, she had a terrible viral infection that had ulcerated her tongue, cheeks, and throat. I knew all about ulcers in the mouth, so I sympathized wholeheartedly with this miserable condition. It took weeks, but slowly Flora healed, and along the way we bonded. Soon, she was a loving, trusting ball of black-and-white fuzz who met me at my door each evening when I returned from work. The loneliness of my apartment vanished, and I cherished the success of our health venture *together*. Although my own future looked uncertain, success with Flora seemed to be something I could achieve.

Only weeks after I'd finally nursed Flora back to some resemblance of healthy kittenhood, she was diagnosed with feline leukemia.

Cancer.

Her veterinarian gave her the same sorry prognosis my oncologist had given me: Flora would most likely die within a year or two.

My response was instant and unconscious. As soon as Flora's vet handed down the diagnosis, I wrote her off as a lost cause. Quickly, my emotional attachment to her ceased as I began to protect myself from the pain of her death, which I knew would come. The veterinarian had told me Flora would die and I simply accepted this; I stopped speaking to Flora and playing with her, because when I did I would end up sobbing hysterically for my kitten. It became difficult for me to even look at her.

But Flora simply wouldn't let me pull away. When I'd walk past her, she'd chase after me. Her paw touched my cheek hesitantly each night as she curled up next to me in bed, her purr resonant and strong. If my mood was chilly, she seemed not to notice. Flora did what cats do best—she waited and watched.

Her patience finally won out. One night I had an *Aha!* experience about my attitude toward Flora. How could I believe my own cancer wasn't a death sentence when I couldn't see the same hope for her? How could I dismiss any being without dismissing myself? Although I was busy blathering about hope and healing, I knew that I honestly saw myself in the grave.

That realization was a profound turning point for me. It was slow in coming, but when it did, it hit me like a downpour of hailstones. How often in my life had I turned away from pain and loss, and from honest feelings? Living a half-life, I'd put away emotion at the first inkling of loss and had nearly lost myself in the process.

One night shortly after my awakening, I lit a candle for Flora and myself. We sat together looking at the flame, and I vowed to Flora that I would love her with wild abandon for as long as she was with me, because loving her felt so good. Pulling away from her hurt, and I didn't need any more painful isolation in my life. In loving Flora, I knew I would find a way to love myself as well—poor diagnosis and all. For the both of us, each day of life would be a day we could celebrate together.

I began a quest to heal Flora that included many of the same gems of complementary medicine I was attempting on myself. Flora got acupressure; vitamins; homeopathy; music and color therapies; detoxifying baths; and unlimited quantities of hugs, love, and affection. Her water bowl had tiny, colorful crystals in it. Her collar was a healing green.

What was most important in this process, though, was the attitude change I experienced from this mumbo-jumbo, as some of my bewildered friends called it. Healing stopped being so painfully heavy. It became fun, even silly. When I told my friends I might have my house visited by dowsers to seek out and correct "bad energy vibrations," I damn well had to have a highly developed sense of humor.

Over the next few months, I slowly learned that healing is more than heroics over illness. Healing isn't simply an end result, it's a process. Flora helped me reclaim the joy that had died after my cancer treatment and my previous relationship had ended. She brought me tremendous peace with her quiet, trusting presence. Finally, as I saw Flora healed, loved, and cherished, I knew I could honestly hold the same hopeful vision for myself.

Flora is sleek, happy, and seven years old today. Her last three tests for leukemia have been negative. At the time of my *Aha!* with Flora, I felt that she was an angel sent to teach me that turning away from love accomplishes nothing. I believe that Flora was ready to die to bring me her message . . . if that's what it would have taken.

—*Susan Chernak McElroy*

Comfort

I was ten years old and the daughter of an alcoholic. I was the only girl in my family and would have felt very isolated and lonely had it not been for my cat Frosty. Sometimes my parents would be gone into the wee hours of the night. My three brothers, who shared a room, would be together doing the things they loved best. Frosty was always beside me keeping me company. We had two other cats in the house in addition to Frosty. My parents were becoming more fed up with the cats every day, and often threatened to get rid of them.

One day I came home from swimming with my friends to find that my parents had given Frosty away. I literally spent the whole night sleepless and in tears, grieving over the pet that had been snatched away from me. My whole life had been shattered. After several weeks, I was still not able to accept the loss of my dearest friend.

One day as I sat on the front porch of my house crying over Frosty, a stray tomcat, who very closely resembled Frosty, appeared out of nowhere. I picked the cat up only to have it reach its paws up and, the best way I can describe it, give me a hug. At the time I felt almost as if Frosty had been returned to me.

The cat, whom I named Harry, stayed around my house keeping me company for many weeks. When I came outside, Harry would instinctively be there ready to play with me. I would spend hours talking to Harry and petting him. Harry helped me work through my grief and feel peace again. Then one day, almost as if Harry knew that my healing had been completed, he suddenly vanished, never to return.

Today when I feel I can't make it through something that is happening in my life, I remember Harry, who came into my life at a time when I had such great need. I know that if I experience loss there will be something that will come and bring me comfort, the way Harry did so long ago.

—*Millie Greer*

The Littlest Counselor

I worked in a crisis house several years back. The people that stayed there were in a lot of emotional and psychological pain.

One day a big old orange tom came to visit us. All

the counselors and the people of the house soon grew to love our Morris (after the famous cat on TV). We all took turns feeding him and worried after him. This was a very rural area and bobcats lived there also. Our supervisor hated cats and said so. She did everything she could to try to get rid of Morris.

My heart would break to see him sitting out in the cold, rainy night on top of a refrigerator looking into the window at us.

Since I was the counselor who held happiness group therapy, I knew how valuable he was to our people at the house. How he could reach them and comfort them like no human ever could.

One particular day, we had a young man, John, come to us who was suffering from a schizophrenia disorder and wanted to leave. He didn't trust any of us so he wouldn't talk to us; he was very frightened. As he was sitting at the picnic table outside, up strolled Morris, who immediately jumped up on the table for a look at John, who turned his head away.

Morris wasn't to be that easily dismissed. He lay down right in front of John and rolled on his back for a scratch on his belly. John reached down with tears in his eyes and petted then held Morris in his arms and talked to him. John had finally found a friend, someone who listened and loved him unconditionally.

I tried very hard to keep Morris with us. After the supervisor said he had to go, we found him another home.

I'll never forget this little feline counselor who helped many people with his caring little spirit and big, loving heart.

—*Roneen Nichols*

Touching

"Now when the sun was setting, all those who had any that were sick with various diseases brought them to him; and he laid his hands on every one of them and healed them." These are timeless words from the apostle Luke. There's something about touching another living being that goes far beyond the mere pressing of flesh to flesh, or fur to fur. When a horse nuzzles another horse on a Texas spread or a cow licks a passing hiker in the Swiss Alps, all time seems to stop. For a few flickering moments, the two creatures are forged together in an inexplicable bond.

What is transmitted in those moments of physical contact no one knows for sure. But somehow the simple act of touching becomes a channel for transformation—a conduit through which the closeness, warmth, and energy of life seem to flow from one being to another.

One of my fondest memories from college was the change that took place in my little kitten, Blue, through a nurturing touch of a frisky puppy. When I first got him, Blue was only five weeks old and had been orphaned before he was weaned from his mother. I had picked him out from a boxful of kittens because I was charmed by his outfit. He was black with little white paws that made him look as if he were dressed in a tuxedo and sneakers.

But as cute as he was, it was clear from the start that he was frightened and unhappy. Often, he would cower in a corner and emit plaintive little mews that were close to a cry. He was desperate to suck on something, *anything*, and he never seemed to be satisfied. Something was missing—and that something was a mother who could comfort and cuddle him.

When my roommates got a new puppy, a mutt they

named Shaboo, Blue's life took on a new dimension. Immediately the two started playing together as though they were brothers. They would chase each other up and down the stairs and whizz around the house at dizzying speed. At mealtimes, they didn't hesitate to eat out of each other's bowl. As they cavorted together, they appeared to be one species: Blue seemed to think Shaboo was a big cat, and Shaboo acted as though Blue were a dog.

I was certain that Blue's newfound happiness came from having a playmate. But I soon discovered that there was also something much deeper going on between this puppy and kitten. One day I came home from school and was startled by a sight that was both incongruous and endearing. There on the living room floor was Blue, nursing on Shaboo's tiny nipples!

Like a mother, Shaboo was lying on his side in quiet repose, looking fondly at the kitten sucking away contentedly. It was an extraordinary scene that made me think of that ancient Roman statue of Romulus and Remus, suckling at the teats of the she-wolf that cared for them when they were abandoned.

Of course, Blue wasn't getting any milk, but that didn't seem to matter to either of them. What did matter was the physical link that had been forged between them—a link that continued to flourish over the eight months they were together. Even as they got older, every day they would cement their bond through the intimate act of touching. They would lie down together for five minutes or so, as big shaggy Shaboo "nursed" his little feline friend.

Through Shaboo's tender act of connecting with Blue, I began to understand that the power of touch is not only founded on the outward, tactile connection between two beings, but is also deeply rooted in the psyche, in the forces of a touch that is caring, enduring, transcendent.

Years later, as a veterinarian making a journey from physical medicine to spiritual understanding, my grasp of these transformational forces deepened. For that, I owe a debt of thanks to an old gray tabby brought into my practice.

The old tabby's pelvis was fractured so badly he couldn't stand. He had been sideswiped by a car, but luckily his fractures were such that they would heal naturally over time without an operation. Although he didn't appear to have any other injuries, it was critical that I keep him in the clinic for a few days just to be sure there was nothing else wrong.

"You don't understand," his owner said pleadingly. "This cat is seventeen and I have another one just like him at home. They were littermates, and they've never been apart a day in their lives. You've got to let me bring him home."

There was no way I could release the cat, no matter how emotionally wrenching the separation might be. Until he was able to stand and had bladder and bowel control, I had no choice but to keep him under observation.

"I'm sorry," I said. "It's best for the cat if he stays."

By the next morning, I wasn't so sure. The tabby gazed into space with such a vacant look in his eye that it seemed he had already given up and died. His vital signs were normal, but there was no life in him. He didn't meow. He didn't purr. He just lay there without eating, staring into some distant place where all hope was extinguished.

As I pondered what to do next, the phone rang. It was the tabby's owner, and he was frantic. "My other cat's been screaming nonstop," he complained. "He never went to sleep—just prowled around searching and meowing. You have to do something."

"I don't know if it will make a difference," I said, "but why don't you bring the other cat here?"

The owner made it to the clinic in twenty minutes. When he walked in with the other cat under his arm, I thought I was seeing double. The brother cat was the image of his littermate—a fluffy pearl gray with stripes. But while his injured sibling lay in a cage torpid in depression, this one was taut with anxious energy.

The minute I opened the cage door, the healing began. The electricity between the two cats was palpable. At the sight of his brother, the ailing cat's eyes brightened, his ears perked up, and he struggled in a futile effort to get up and draw near to him.

But it was his brother's caring touch that really made the injured cat come alive. He bounded into the cage, rushed up to his brother, and meowing with joy, began licking and sniffing him all over. With the all-important physical link reestablished, the hurt cat mewed in response, and mustering all of his strength, reciprocated by licking any part of his brother's body that brushed by him. A leg, a tail, an ear, a shoulder—all were touched by his tongue.

The two cats couldn't seem to get enough of each other. They kept licking, and cleaning, and smelling, oblivious to anything but each other. They made it clear that for the rest of the clinic stay, they would be in the cage together.

That night, I peeked into the cage and saw that the cats were still inseparable. They were huddled close together, purring in unison, as the brother cat encircled his hurt twin with the loving warmth of his body.

After about three days, the hurt cat began to have normal bowel movements and had regained bladder control, which suggested that he had no further significant internal injuries. By the fourth day, he was able to stand on his own, with the help of his brother. The brother nudged him with his nose a few times, and the injured cat got the message. Haltingly, he struggled to his feet, leaning briefly against his brother for support. A few seconds later, he stood proudly on his own and took a few wobbly steps.

The next day, they went home. I didn't see them again until two years later, when they came in for a checkup. By then, they were nineteen and still in good health. The injured cat had fully recovered and never showed any ill effects of the accident. The healing had resulted not from some medical breakthrough or traditional veterinary science, but from the tender touch of a brother, whose physical acts of love helped bring about the recovery.

Observing interactions like the one involving the two tabbies, I have been impressed by how powerful and far-reaching caring physical contact can be. In particular, I'm reminded of research that has documented the importance of an attitude of caring in human healing through the laying on of hands. Dolores Krieger, a former New York University professor of nursing, conducted pioneering studies on the subject back in the early 1970s and discovered that patients who were treated by the laying on of hands had a higher hemoglobin count—the pigment in the bloodstream that carries life-giving oxygen to the cells—than those without such treatment.

Clearly, something positive is happening within the body when a patient is touched. However, this salutary physiological response doesn't necessarily correlate with healing. Searching for the curative secret in a simple touch, Krieger discovered that what counted most was whether or not the nurses *cared* about their patients. In some mysterious way, that caring attitude was transferred through the nurse's hands to the patient and thereby stimulated a healing response.

That's what I seem to have witnessed with the two tabbies—a profound caring that had been transferred from one to the other through the touch of a tongue. And that physical contact had brought the gift of life.

—Allen M. Schoen

CHAPTER NINE

Mystery and Mischief

All right, said the Cat; and this time it vanished quite slowly, beginning with the end of the tail, and ending with the grin, which remained some time after the rest of it had gone.

Lewis Carroll, *Alice in Wonderland*

Some years ago we lived in England and I had several encounters with one of the better minds of our time. I. J. Good of Oxford has been one of this century's signal contributors to both physics and statistics. . . . Somehow precognition came up and I asked him if he had ever thought much about it. Without hesitation he acknowledged he had had many such experiences himself and startled me by saying the explanation was really quite simple. "We have found," he said in his cultured Oxford tones, "that there are subatomic particles that move around the nuclei of their respective atoms in the wrong direction. Now," Jack said, "if the basic building blocks of matter itself can run backwards, for that is what they are surely doing, so can time. It has to be so. When you are precognitive, you are simply remembering the future." To the point: can that be applied to the cat? . . . Can time run backwards for cats as well as people?

Roger Caras

The Ballad of Norma Jean

In a city I once lived in, there's a story of a remarkable cat. It sounds like one of those urban myths but I can assure you it is true. I know the people involved. I know the cats involved. It is a story our family tells. We call it "The Ballad of Norma Jean."

Margot occupied the rear half of a modest duplex. She was thrilled to discover that the new tenant for the front half was an old school friend of hers, Laura. Margot was already owned and operated by two felines and it didn't take her long to convince Laura she needed a cat of her own.

Laura found a delicate Siamese half-breed kitten at the humane society. She named the cat Mishkit and was so pleased with her that she went back to the humane society to find a second cat to keep Mishkit company when Laura was at work.

This time she brought home a gorgeous white longhaired cat with a dramatic and vampy personality. Her name? Norma Jean.

Norma Jean settled in beautifully and became a well-known fixture as she loved to stretch out on the front steps and queen it over the neighborhood.

But all too quickly Margot moved across town and lost touch with Laura. A short while later, Laura bought a house and she also moved out of the duplex with her two new cats.

Cats often hate to move, but Mishkit adjusted easily. Norma Jean, however, did not make the move with such good grace. She sulked, she stopped eating, stopped cleaning herself, and made her displeasure known in all those charming ways cats have of expressing themselves. Laura was quick to take her to the vet, convinced the cat was suffering some kind of physical ailment. Many treatments and dollars later Norma Jean's behavior had not changed and the vet strongly recommended an animal psychiatrist.

Various subtle behavior modification programs were attempted, to no avail. Norma Jean only worsened. She began attacking Mishkit. Now Laura had *two* miserable cats. Norma Jean was filthy and thin. Mishkit was on tranquilizers.

Laura gave up hope and began calling friends to find Norma Jean a new home. Perhaps Laura's friends knew Norma Jean too well: No one offered to take the cat. Laura called me at this time but with four cats of my own I couldn't help her. She tearfully told me she was going to have to take Norma Jean back to the humane society. The only good news was that the society agreed to give Norma Jean back to Laura if she was not adopted within a week. This was no great consolation, but Laura felt she had no alternative.

I talked with her shortly thereafter and asked after Norma Jean. Laura still felt guilty about the cat but was very pleased to say that she had been adopted less than three days after she had been returned to the humane society.

Margot knew nothing of these developments, only that Laura had moved away. So she was very surprised when one day, as she bicycled through her old neighborhood, she saw an elegant long-haired white cat sunning on Norma Jean's old front steps. Had she been misinformed? Maybe Laura hadn't moved after all. So she stopped, rang the doorbell, and inquired after Laura. A stranger answered the door. He had occupied the apartment for many months, and no, he did not know the previous tenant. Margot was very confused by now and worried that Norma Jean had run away from Laura and returned to her old haunts. So she asked the (very patient) stranger if the cat had been in situ when he had moved in.

Here the fellow became enthusiastic. He told Margot that this was a very special, extraordinary cat. He and his wife had adopted her from the humane society a while ago. They had brought the sickly, frightened cat home and were amazed when the animal displayed a preternatural familiarity with the apartment and the neighborhood. They had never seen an animal recover and adapt so quickly.

The cat's name? Norma Jean.

It was only when Margot finally tracked Laura down that the full story emerged, to much relief and amazement on everyone's part.

It has been several years since I moved from the city where these events took place. For all I know you may still be able to see Norma Jean lounging on her steps, lording it over the neighborhood. It would be just like her.

—*Nancy Ruth Jackson*

Subway's Wild Ride

Four years ago, my brother walked in the house with a little kitten. Life immediately became a roller-coaster ride, and Subway was his name. Subway was a beautifully marked orange tabby with a very happy, if a little devilish, personality. Subway loved his early-morning romps in the countryside, which often started at 4:00. Living in our rural area, he'd have a ball running, climbing, hunting—and bringing home little treats for Grandma and Grandpa. Chipmunks, mice, moles, garden snakes, birds, bunnies, even a squirrel decorated our driveway. When he wasn't hunting, Subway was a mischievous character who loved to chase butterflies, drink water from the birdbath, and tease our golden retriever, Snickers.

One morning two years ago, Subway didn't come back from his morning jag, and we were heartbroken. Hours later we found him under a bush, and we rushed him to a veterinarian—Subway had been hit with a shotgun blast! Miraculously, he survived. Even with sixteen bullet fragments lodged in his hind legs and torso, Subway couldn't wait for his morning romp.

Unfortunately, we mere mortals spent many a gray light before dawn waiting for Subway and wishing he'd come home. One morning, we realized our worst fears. Our beloved cat didn't come home! On their way to the market, Grandma and Grandpa found Subway lying on the side of the road. Shocked and upset, they got a box and a shovel and carried him home for a dignified burial in our backyard. Grandma called my brother, who had brought Subway into our lives, and asked him to help. My brother came and held Grandma as she cried. The next hour felt like days as they prepared the box and the grave, Grandma shedding tears every step of the way. As the time came near to say their good-byes, across the yard came a blur of orange fur, no doubt wondering what all the excitement was, what he was missing. He was missing his own funeral! Grandma wiped away her tears and stood in shock yelling, "Subby! He's alive! He's alive!"

I guess you could say this was a Subway that arrived a little late.

—Margaret Carroll

The Dream

During a long period of disability my brother gave me a black-and-white kitten, whom I named Pokey. We became best of friends through thick and thin. Though my husband was allergic to cats, I insisted that Pokey and I were a package deal.

Pokey and I were together for seven years until he became very ill with liver disease. The vet assured me it would be wise to put an end to his suffering. As I held him in my arms I told him that since cats had nine lives, he would always be welcome to return to me. I thanked him for the joy he had brought to my life and told him that I would always love him very much. As I hugged him, I realized that he was gone. I hoped that he heard my final words.

I was very distraught about Pokey's death, and about six months after he died I had a peculiar dream. As big as if he were human, Pokey was sitting with me at a sidewalk café in Paris. We were sipping coffee.

With his cup in one enormous paw, he extended the other to cover my hand and said, "Look for the gray cat with orange ears." Startled, I woke up and told my husband about the dream. I said I had never seen a gray-and-orange cat before and I didn't think they came in that color scheme. Concurring, he went back to sleep.

Only a few times during the next several years did I give the dream any thought. I concluded that I missed Pokey very much and concocted this dream to help me cope with losing such a good friend. By 1994 the dream was almost totally forgotten.

On a warm day in June of that year my husband and I took a walk to enjoy the breeze. As we approached an area of dense ornamental brush I heard the faint cries of a helpless kitten. I crawled under the bushes and found the baby next to the trunk of a tall tree. It was dark in the underbrush, but I looked to be sure there were no more kittens. Sure that she was the only one there, I realized that her hip was broken, probably from someone tossing her away like trash. Very carefully I cupped her in my hands and crawled out of the foliage, making sure not to cause her any pain. There in the light I realized that I held a gray cat with orange ears.

This story still amazes me. We still have the gray cat with orange ears, and we love her dearly. She lives happily with our Siamese, our black cat, and our two dogs. She visits elderly residents at a nearby retirement home and is the joy of one resident in particular. She is, in every way we can imagine, the fulfillment of Pokey's dream. I'm glad we were directed to look for her.

—*Mary Sullivan*

Carmel and Bobby—
Together Again

Sue Blocher of Brookline, Massachusetts, will always remember that day in September 1977 when her son, Bobby, then four years old, came running up to her in the kitchen, where she was busy baking oatmeal cookies, and asked breathlessly, "Please, Mommy, oh, please! Can it sleep with me?"

"Can what sleep with you? Big Bird? Kermit the Frog? Miss Piggy?"

Bobby giggled. "No, Mommy, no! Can my kitty sleep with me tonight?"

Sue arched an eyebrow and wiped a piece of cookie dough off the edge of the bowl.

"But, honey boy," she said, puzzled. "You don't have a kitty."

"I do now, Mommy," Bobby replied confidently. "A pretty *carmel*-colored kitty, just like before. Daddy is bringing her home to me. I saw him buy it."

Darn it! Sue's smile became more like a grimace. Bobby was always doing things like this to her. What did he mean, "a carmel-colored kitty just like before"?

And had he really seen Edward buying him a cat?

Well, she would know the answer to the second question very soon. Her husband was due home from Boston a little after 5:00 P.M.

Bobby went out to play, and Sue went back to her cookies.

At 5:08, Edward Blocher pulled into their driveway —with a kitten in the car.

Neither Sue nor Edward had ever seen their son so elated. They were touched by his repeated tearful thank-you's, but bewildered by his triumphant shout, "Oh, yes! It's Bobby and Carmel—together again!"

In the next few weeks, boy and kitten were seldom apart. And they did sleep together every night.

In December, Gail, Bobby's baby sister, was born. Bobby and Carmel were at the door to greet her when Sue and Edward brought her home from the hospital.

Gently nudging his Grandmother Linzer aside, Bobby beamed and said to his cat, "See, Carmel. Little Gail. Just like before."

Edward and Sue exchanged puzzled glances; and later that evening, while they sat at the dinner table talking over the excitement of the day, Sue asked what Bobby had meant by saying "just like before."

Bobby shrugged, moving the tip of a finger through a spot of gravy on his plate. "Like before. You know, like before when Carmel, Gail, and I were together."

Edward laughed at his ever-imaginative son, but his mother-in-law glowered at them.

"Such silly talk!" Grandmother Linzer said. "Susan, I've warned you before that you should not permit Robert to chatter on so about such nonsense."

"Mother," Sue reminded the older woman, "Bobby won't be five for another six months. He's a little kid. Little kids sometimes say weird things."

"You never did," her mother said with a sniff. "And remember, as the twig is bent, so grows the branch."

As they were preparing for bed, Sue, fatigued from the birth, asked her husband to pass her the baby *chowder*, rather than the powder.

Edward teasingly reminded her that she never said "weird things."

Sue laughed. She agreed with her mother's observation that she had been a perfect child, then, turning serious, asked her husband what he made of Bobby's frequent references to "before"—first with Carmel and now with his new sister.

"Maybe he had wanted a cat for so long and so

badly that it seemed to him as though he had already had the cat when I finally did bring it to him, and maybe the same thing is true about Gail," Edward said. "Or maybe it's just what you said—kids say weird things."

Life proceeded on its normal, somewhat hectic course in the Blocher household. Edward received a promotion, and things became more comfortable and less chaotic. They still didn't have enough extra money to allow for more than an occasional night out, but Sue didn't mind, since she hated to leave her children in the care of a baby-sitter.

As for Bobby and Carmel, Sue was convinced that boy and cat communicated on some level beyond the ordinary. At first she had worried that the tight union between Bobby and Carmel would not allow an intruder, but her fears proved unwarranted. Both Bobby and Carmel appeared to adore baby Gail, and they played with her whenever Sue permitted it.

It was just before Bobby's seventh birthday that Sue's and Edward's universe became quite a bit larger.

At quarter to three in the morning, they were awakened by their son's loud weeping. They both ran to his room.

"I don't want Carmel to die," he said between convulsive sobs. "I don't want her to die again!"

The cat looked up at them from her nest in Bobby's bedspread. Her large green eyes appeared to glow in the dim illumination from the Donald Duck nightlight near the bedroom door.

"Carmel is fine, Slugger," Edward said softly. "You were just having a bad dream."

"No." Bobby shook his head. "Tomorrow I'll be seven. I don't want Carmel to die like before."

"Bobby, what is this 'before' business again?" Sue asked.

"Like before when the wolf tried to eat Gail! Carmel and I fought and fought to save her, but the wolf killed Carmel—and nearly killed me!"

Edward shook his head and laughed. "Wow! My man, what did you have for a snack before you went to bed? Whatever it was, you are never eating it again!"

Sue stayed at Bobby's bedside, holding his hand until he went back to sleep.

The next afternoon Sue was in the kitchen frosting the birthday cake for Bobby's party.

Her mother was in the backyard with Gail and Bobby.

Edward was still at work, but was expected home any minute.

At 5:30, the Murchisons, the Quateros, and the Fanellis would be bringing their children over for the party.

In Sue's mind, everyone was accounted for, and her world was an orderly place.

What she hadn't counted on was the large German shepherd that had somehow entered their yard.

"Shoo, you dog!" Sue heard her mother scolding. "You don't belong in here, you nasty thing! Get out. Shoo! Shoo!"

Then, as Sue watched in horror through the kitchen window, she saw the shepherd lunge at her mother. Grandmother Linzer screamed, stepped backward, and tripped over a picnic bench, dropping baby Gail.

Sue's mouth opened in a silent scream as her worst nightmare came to life—and she seemed helpless to do anything to stop it. In absolute dread she watched the German shepherd moving toward Gail as if someone had thrown him a tasty chunk of meat.

And then, from out of nowhere, Carmel flew at the big dog's muzzle, scratching, hissing, biting—a veritable guardian angel with claws.

And Bobby was there. Her beautiful, valiant, seven-year-old son was striking at the monstrous dog with the little red plastic bat he had received on his sixth birthday.

"Not like before! Not like before! Not like before!" Bobby chanted in rhythm with the stinging swats he delivered to the snarling dog that threatened his sister.

Bobby's words from the night before echoed in Sue's brain: *"Carmel and I fought and fought to save her, but the wolf killed Carmel!"*

Could it be true? Were Bobby and Carmel fighting the wolf all over again?

"Bobby and Carmel—together again!"

The huge dog shook his head vigorously and sent Carmel flying against the side of the house. The cat was dazed from the blow, but she rolled to her feet and once again advanced on the intruder.

Somehow Bobby had got astride the shepherd and was pulling the dog's ears with all his strength.

The distraction was all Carmel needed. This time, she went for the giant's eyes. She was a demon out of hell as well as a guardian angel.

The German shepherd shook Bobby off, got the boy on his back, and tried to sink his fangs into Bobby's throat. Bobby cried out in pain as the dog's teeth tore pieces of flesh from his chest.

Her master's screams brought a frenzied power to Carmel's attack. Mercilessly she sank her claws into the dog's left eye.

Emitting terrible yowls of pain, the shepherd tried desperately to shake the screaming cat from its face.

By the time Carmel had once again been thrown against a wall, Sue was there with an iron frying pan. As if Carmel's feline fighting spirit had possessed her, she struck at the big dog's head again and again.

The German shepherd was dazed and barely alive

when he staggered from the Blochers' yard. Within the hour, an animal control unit had the dog in custody.

Bobby missed his birthday party. He had to have some stitches and a few shots.

Carmel had a broken back leg that had to be set between splints.

Baby Gail and Grandmother Linzer were unharmed.

And as Bobby said as he hugged his cat on the way home from the veterinarian, "Bobby and Carmel—together again!"

Neither Sue nor Edward asked what he meant. Whether their son had some memory of a past life or had experienced a kind of premonition, it really didn't matter. They only knew for certain that love—whether between human beings or between human beings and animals—lasts forever.

—*Brad Steiger*

Willie or Won't He?

It was a mild December evening in Doylestown, Pennsylvania, so mild, in fact, we were barbecuing dinner on the patio. Willie, our eleven-year-old black-and-white cat, must have slipped out then. We never noticed his absence, even though he always begged for food at dinner. I guess we were preoccupied with our adorable new Abyssinian kitten, who was, as usual, putting on his cute kitten show.

My husband and I visited friends that evening, and when we returned, we called for Willie to come to bed. He always slept with me at night and obediently responded to my nighttime ritual call. That night, he did not come when I called. We took to the streets of our neighborhood, armed with flashlights. No Willie!

Willie was having trouble adjusting to the new kitten, but I never thought sibling rivalry would come to this.

The next morning, Willie did not return. While driving our youngest child to school, only two miles from home, I saw a black-and-white cat along the roadside. As I did not want my son to see, I took him to school, and returned to the spot without him. I pulled the car over, and looked at the body. It looked like Willie.

With tears in my eyes, I drove to work in my husband's office. We had an office party planned that day. However, I had my husband cancel it, and we went together to pick up Willie from alongside the road. We buried him along the creek in a beautiful spot. We truly loved him.

After eleven days, the weather had turned very cold. The ground was icy, and patches of snow littered the lawns. We finally had a break in the weather, and my sons opened the garage door and were playing outside. As I was making dinner, I heard a horrible wailing sound coming from the garage. The sound became louder and more plaintive. I ran to the door, wondering what the commotion was.

Willie had returned, his beautifully groomed white hair gray from dirt.

After drinking two full bowls of water, and eating

the best tuna fish in the house, Willie was back. I guess he wanted to show us that we had buried the wrong cat!

Willie lived to a ripe old age of twenty-one and a half and got over his sibling rivalry after he made his decision to come home.

—*Judi Blumenthal*

The Second Coming of Thumpy

One summer evening, when she was eighteen years old, Thumpy jumped into my lap, and stared at me with her old green eyes for a long time. We had an unspoken language between us. But I was feeling fine that evening; Thumpy was saying something else. A chill passed over me, and I had the feeling Thumpy was telling me she was about to leave us.

That night, old Thumpy died in her sleep. It was a dark day at our house. My husband and I cried and held each other for a long time. It was so hard to accept that such a loyal, wonderful companion of so many years could suddenly be gone.

Thumpy was a wise old cat who ruled our roost for almost two decades and slept at the foot of our bed, nipping our toes if we dared disturb her sleep. For years she had been a crabby cat who loved jumping into empty cartons more than anything else in the world. But when our four children entered our lives Thumpy was remarkably gentle with them, never nipping, always tolerant of the ministrations of toddlers, even though Thumpy was always our first child.

Five days after her passing, I was about to discard an empty TV carton, when I decided to keep it until the thirty-day warranty had passed. I left the box in the archway between the living room and dining room, thinking aloud, "If Thumpy were alive I couldn't leave this here. She'd be trying to get in it and set off the alarm." Our one and only motion detector for our home security system sits on an end table in direct line with the archway.

Thinking no more about it, we set the alarm that night and went to sleep. At two in the morning we were nearly blasted out of our bed by the shrieking siren and were downstairs in a flash. The doors were all locked, and nothing had been disturbed.

From that day on I no longer cried about Thumpy. When our eight-year-old daughter mentioned some days later that she had seen Thumpy cross the kitchen and disappear near the stove, I knew our beloved cat was still with us, still getting into mischief!

—*Margaret M. Litt*

Kitty Calling

According to legend, cats are unpredictable. But several years ago, our family learned that one old rule of thumb holds true for felines as for their humanfolk: the apple never falls far from the tree.

Someone was answering the phone when we weren't home.

"I called your house, but who answered?" puzzled friends would say. "Someone picked up the phone, but all I heard was a cat meowing."

It didn't take long to narrow the suspects to our four-year-old cat, Heartsey. We had installed a telephone on the wall in the hallway near the teenagers' bedrooms. Under that phone was the clothes hamper.

If no one was home when the phone rang, Heartsey appointed herself the family's personal secretary. She jumped on the hamper, pawed the receiver off the hook, and then "spoke" into the mouthpiece. This also solved the mystery of who was leaving the phone off the hook numerous times.

A gift for using human technology runs in Heartsey's family. Heartsey's late mom, who used to live with the family next door, didn't bother scratching or meowing at the door when she wanted to go inside. She jumped on the ledge by the front door, lifted her paw and rang the doorbell.

—*Barbara Darling*

The Laugh

A month after my father's funeral, we adopted a tiny sickly kitten who had been found abandoned in an alleyway in a poor section of town with his littermates. We promptly named him Nails, the nickname of an aggressive, tobacco-chewing, perpetually dirt-covered pro baseball player in our city. My son saw the similarities immediately.

Nails introduced himself to us by stepping over the heads of his well-behaved sisters to meow mightily in our faces. He was loud and dirty, and if he wasn't yowling he was sneezing. I picked him up and didn't put him down until we got home. At the approximate age of five weeks, he immediately took over the house.

Nails quickly grew from a tiny, sick kitten into a sleek hunter who is bossy and arbitrary; a demolisher of window screens; a slob who beats his food to death on the kitchen floor before he eats it; a romeo hopelessly in love with our sophisticated lady cat, Maggie (who won't have a thing to do with him); a bully who feels entitled to sit in a dinner plate and remain unrepentant; and a brawler who will bite my husband for any provocation, including gentle petting (and remain unrepentant). Nails has been labeled "psycho" by my nieces, costs us a nice piece of change at the vets, has all the finesse of Tony Perkins in the shower, and is a healer of the hearts. Nails is the love object of an eighty-four-year-old widow, a fourteen-year-old girl, and a seventeen-year-old boy—and last Halloween night, he gave me a gift beyond my imaginings.

He let me hear the laughter of my father.

I was sitting with Nails that evening, working at my desk in the old bedroom where my father died. My mother had been unable to sleep in that bedroom after my father passed away and we'd converted the bedroom into a sitting room. Mom had moved down the hall into a smaller bedroom and with her knitting, armchair, and Nails to keep her company she seemed content. Mom was away that evening, All Hallows' Eve.

I was concentrating on my work with the TV news on only as background noise, when I stopped to watch a Halloween segment on ghosts hosted by a local anchor. The newsman was interviewing a psychic. I parked myself in an old armchair, and Nails jumped into my lap. Now, my father was a man who had no time for silly things like ghosts and psychics; he was an old engineer and a very practical sort. Nor had I had any inkling of his presence in the house—or anywhere —after his death. I didn't then, either, until the show ended and I spoke out loud.

"Well, what do you think, Dad—still no ghosts?"

With that, Nails jumped from my lap and flew to the floor, his back arched, spitting. He glared to the side of the room and backed out, still arched, hissing all the way. I turned and looked and saw nothing, but then I heard a laugh, and it was Dad's laugh. There was nothing frightening about the incident, in fact, after a moment I started laughing too. I'd think of it as an incident born of an overactive imagination, but for Nails and his reaction. Nails has never hissed or arched his back before or since. Now I think of the laugh as a gift, and Nails as its bearer.

—*Patris Spanos*

CHAPTER TEN

Love and Death

They say when you die and go to heaven all the dogs and cats you've ever had in your life come running to meet you. Until that day, rest in peace.

Kinky Friedman

The Best Cat Ever

I remember well—as I'm sure anyone who has ever been owned by a cat always does—the first time I knew Polar Bear was seriously ill. I remember it well—as I'm sure you remember when you knew your cat was seriously ill. It is like being stabbed.

I also remember the first time I recognized that it was something far worse than either arthritis or the mere inevitable gradual encroachment of old age. I was playing chess with Ed Kunz—a Swiss gentleman and close friend of mine who lives in the same apartment building. Polar Bear was, as usual, lying asleep beside me on my chair, and I was leaning over to pat him from time to time.

But chess is a very absorbing game, and one time, when I had not looked at him for some moments and reached out to pat him, I suddenly realized he was not there. At almost the same moment—or at least so it seemed to me—he hit the floor. Or, rather, what he really did was to flop to the floor. It was a sad and awful sight. Worst of all, as I picked him up, he looked at me as if to apologize.

Animals battle whatever infirmity or wound or disability they have with such bravery and lack of complaining that it must actually be seen to believed. I would see that quality in Polar Bear many times that terrible spring, and I shall never forget it. Every now and then, I would hear one of his small *AEIOU's*—the sound with which I had grown so lovingly familiar—and the only difference I could notice now was that it was a little eerily cut short, until it sounded almost like a plain *ow*. It was not, of course, but that is what it sounded like.

Anyone who has ever been in a position similar to

mine and who has seen his or her animal carry on a
difficult fight can only love and respect that animal
more, particularly when you realize that it takes a very
special kind of courage. It takes a courage that is very
different from human courage but is, if anything, more
worthy of admiration, because human courage comes
at least armed with some knowledge, whereas animal
courage often comes with no knowledge at all—not
even, in the case of disease, knowledge of what it is
they fight.

In any case, after that awful flop to the floor, I knew
it was high time, and probably past high time, for me to
take Polar Bear to the vet.

Polar Bear was, as are almost all cats, extremely
wary of a vet office and regarded it at best as somewhere between a Lebanon and an Iraq. Although his
vet, Dr. Fred Tierney, could not have been more gentle or considerate, I could tell from his first examina-
tion of Polar Bear that he was concerned. When he was
finished, I knew from the look in his eye that the news
was not good. And it certainly was not. What Polar
Bear had was that dreaded age-old disease that eventually afflicts so many animals: uremic poisoning, or kidney failure.

I cannot even now bring myself to go over the day-
after-day, week-after-week, step-by-steps Dr. Tierney
tested and tried: the treatments that sometimes seemed
to make Polar Bear suddenly better and then—equally
suddenly, it seemed—failed as well as those that
seemed, at first, and oh so slowly, to help a little and
then, just as slowly, seemed to fail. Finally, there came
the day when Dr. Tierney said quietly, "I am beginning to wonder whether we're doing the little fellow
much of a favor."

I did not answer, but I knew the answer.

If there was one thing about which I was determined, it was that Polar Bear should not suffer pain. I hate to see any animal in pain, but for the cat who had probably done as much as any single cat who ever lived for the cause of cats in general and the adoption of strays in particular—and had done it not only in this country but also in nineteen other countries where the books about him were published—for that cat to suffer pain was simply, to me, unconscionable.

The next morning, I sent for Polar Bear's close friends to say good-bye to him—among them every single one of the staff and volunteers from the Fund for Animals office. Each one of them held him in his or her lap and hugged him.

Vets are not always keen on having the owners hold their animal or even being in the same room when their animal is being put down. The reason is that most vets have had experiences with it that do not make it practicable—experiences ranging from hysterics to last-minute changes of mind.

In my case, I was pleased that Dr. Tierney never even mentioned this. He knew, without my saying it, not only that I wanted to be in the room with Polar Bear but also that I wanted to be holding him.

The first injection was an anesthetic, but then before the final one, the sodium pentobarbital, something happened that I shall never forget. Polar Bear was lying on a metal-topped table, and I was holding his head with both my hands. Marian, my longtime assistant, had her hands on him too, but just before the final injection—with what must have been for him, considering his condition, incredible effort—he pushed in a kind of swimming movement on the metal directly toward me. I knew he was trying to get to me, and although Dr. Tierney was already administering the fatal shot, I bent my face down to meet that last valiant effort of his, and with both my hands hugged him as hard as I could.

In what seemed just a few seconds, it was all over. Dr. Tierney did a last check. "He's gone," he said, still quietly. Only then did I release my hugging hold, but as I say, I still remember that last effort of his, and I shall remember it always.

Actually, leaving the room, I was good at first. When I got to the outer office, however, I saw Dorsey Smith—a dear friend of mine and Polar Bear's too— who was holding her own cat in her hands.

"Is it Polar Bear?" she asked me. I nodded. But when she also asked, "Is he all right?" I could not even shake my head. Instead I did something so un-Bostonian and so un-me—something I could not help, not even just in front of Dorsey but with all those other patients there too. I burst into tears. It was embarrassing, and I was ashamed; but the worst part was that for the first time in my life that I can remember, I could not stop crying.

I have always believed that the best place to bury your animals is in your heart. But at the same time, since so many people knew Polar Bear and wanted to know where he would be buried, I finally gave in. I chose as his final resting place the Fund for Animals' Black Beauty Ranch in Murchison, Texas, which over the years has become home to thousands of abused or abandoned animals.

To Chris Byrne, the able manager of the ranch, as well as to his extraordinary wife, Mary, fell the job of finding the right place, the right headstone, the right plaque. They did it wonderfully well. The plaque is not only a lovely one but also is at the very center of life at the ranch and is in the shade of three trees —a place that Polar Bear loved.

To me fell the job of writing the inscription for the plaque. I did it as follows:

Beneath This Stone
Lie the Mortal Remains of
The Cat Who Came for Christmas
Beloved Polar Bear
1977–1992
'Til We Meet Again

What I wrote on Polar Bear's monument I do believe—that we will meet again. And if I do not always believe it, I always try to believe it, because I also believe that if you try hard enough to believe something, you will in time believe it. And one thing I know is that, when Polar Bear and I do meet again, the first thing I will say to him is that he is the best cat ever. And another thing I know is that, wherever we are, he will be the best cat there too.

—*Cleveland Amory*

Death of the Old Cat

Coaldust willed the walk into the wild part out back, across the bridge, set herself adrift from forced feeding and needles hooked to water bags. Like old ones among Eskimos, she launched herself free to solitude on ice floes. I tried to stop her, as if I could.

Later, she left the woods, walked tentatively back across the bridge, and ascended the veranda, her favorite summer place. She sprung light as a black cricket, my old tortoiseshell girl, drifted into the cushioned wicker chair, and lay wispy as breezes against the pillow. Each sickly black-and-brown hair separated in the wind, showing pink skin. I wanted to help her, as if I could.

Under the big pine, we fed her more baby-food meat, and glucose. She struggled against our hope. I cradled her back to the porch, set her upright, and watched her wilt onto the planks. I said no, involuntarily, and placed my hand on her hollow stomach, feeling the last breaths of twelve years together. As if I could, I let her go.

My husband's dull shovel rings against rocky soil out back. I sit cross-legged like a child beside Coaldust on the veranda floor, keeping away the blue fly, chatting with her about how easy she was to live with. She only mouthed meows like a ventriloquist's doll. Her bicolored eyes of yellow and gold I will not forget, as if I could.

—*Deborah Clifford Gessaman*

Rosemary's Cat Who Came
for Christmas

I met my best friend, Mittens, my cat, at Christmastime 1993. My son had originally bought this calico kitten, but he decided that he didn't have the time for her and asked me to take her in.

I said yes, but I felt resentful. I was at a stage in my life that I didn't want to deal with any more responsibility, not even for a tiny cat. I had lost a beloved uncle, my father, and my mother to cancer that year. I was feeling so low I didn't even think I had anything to give to anyone—not even an animal.

This kitten was adorable, big as a minute and only five weeks old. From the first day, every time I looked at her, I would say, "I'm not sure you're staying, so don't get too comfortable!" One day, I was sitting on my sofa looking over Christmas cards from the year before. Mittens was making her way over to me. I came across a card from my mother, and I began to cry. I felt this little kitten climbing up my pants leg, and then she made her way onto my chest. As though she were trying to comfort me, she began to lick each tear from my face. I had to smile, and I said to her, "Okay, you're in!"

—*Rosemary Macklin*

Sea of Love

About twelve years ago, my boyfriend and I were dining at a beachside restaurant in Clearwater Beach, Florida. At our table outside was a sweet, furry black cat, barefoot and pregnant, demurely accepting any seafood offerings that came her way. The owners of the establishment told us she was a stray and that because she had no home, her kittens would most likely die shortly after birth.

I was so saddened. This kitty needed me, and soon! I was also taken with her. She bore tremendous likeness to my dear cat Samantha, who had recently passed away from a two-year bout with feline leukemia.

After dinner, we decided that we had much pent-up love to give away now that Samantha was gone. So I gathered the kitty up, and we put her in the car and took her home with us. She did not fight or cry; she wanted to come. After all, she had really picked us.

Indy—short for Indira—had her kittens a few days later. We worked hard to find them homes, but we kept Indy. She was my best friend and closest companion. My boyfriend left but Indy stayed. She traveled with me to San Francisco and then to Miami, as I searched for the perfect place to live. She always listened to my problems with understanding and without complaint. She saw boyfriends come and go; she also met and befriended the one that stayed and became my husband.

Last September, I noticed that Indy was listless and wasn't eating. We took her to the family vet, but he couldn't find anything conclusive. After a week of testing at an animal hospital, Indy was diagnosed with lymphatic cancer. She had only a week or so to live. We were devastated, but she spent her last days at home with us. Our drive to the animal hospital was very sad, but we cherished that last drive in the car together; Indy always loved car rides.

About a week later, when my husband returned to the animal hospital to pick up Indy's ashes, the doctor told him that someone had abandoned two kittens in their parking lot that morning. Was he interested in giving one, or both, a good home?

My husband called me and we decided, yes, we had much pent-up love to give away since Indy had passed on. He put the kittens, Moonshadow and Droog, in the car and took them home. Like Indy, the kittens love car rides, and we take them everywhere, even on vacation.

A week to the hour after Indy's death, we bought a bottle of good champagne, got on our bicycles, and rode to the beach with her ashes. We did a toast to Indy and sat on the beach until the champagne was gone and the sun had vanished. I sang "Sea of Love" while putting her ashes into the ocean. ("Do you remember when we met? That's the day I knew you were my pet. I want to tell you how much I love you.") Then we went home and looked at old pictures and videos of Indy when she was happy and healthy, while Moonshadow and Droog sat on our laps and looked on.

When we sail the waters in our sailboat, she will forever be under our bow.

—*Carrie F. Bekker*

Pa and Leo

Pa was just fine over Labor Day. We took a trip to our hometown, Leadville, Colorado. We left Leo the cat home. He was always good about staying alone over a weekend with plenty of food and water.

Pa got a toothache in mid September. He went to the dentist—the dentist found a small tumor in his jaw and sent him to an oral surgeon. The surgeon removed the tumor—malignant. He said tumors don't start in jaws—a lung X-ray nine months before was clean. This lung X-ray and bone scan showed a lot—a mass in the lungs—spread to the groin and to the chest.

On Friday the 13th of October the doctor told Pa he had maybe a month, a year, or five years to live. Leo knew too—he was very sad. He quit eating. He, too, had a toothache. The vet tested him—cancer, he said.

Pa died in November, of cancer.

Leo died in early December, of cancer—but Leo also died of a broken heart because Pa and Leo were inseparable.

So they both went to heaven together and are still inseparable. Those of us left here on earth miss them both terribly. But we know they are happy and without pain and looking down at us from above.

—*Deanna Leino*

The Rainbow Bridge

I am a volunteer at the North Carolina State University Veterinary School in Raleigh, North Carolina. Our organization is called Friends Helping Friends. All pets seen at the school have been referred by their local veterinarian, so the problems are fairly serious. I work in the waiting room, where I greet and talk to the four-legged patients and their two-legged mommies and daddies who bring them in. We try to make both the four-legged and two-legged kind feel at ease.

I have a twelve-year-old Labrador, Shadow, and starting with the start of the new television season last year, she has become a critic. After a few minutes of listening to TV she gets up and goes into the bedroom. She may have more sense than my wife and I do.

I have always loved animals, and I understand the tremendous feelings people share with me every day. It makes me feel better, knowing I'm helping people through their feelings of loss, which are universal. Someday I know someone will help me when I need it.

In addition to the waiting room in our clinic, we also have a Quiet Room, where we or the vet talk to the people in the event of a worst-case scenario. There are two essential things given out should a pet die. They are "Prayer at the Death of a Pet," and "The Rainbow Bridge."

These are classics that are handed from pet lover to pet lover in a chain of caring and support. This chain keeps growing and growing as our society recognizes more and more the profound ways our best friends enrich our lives and remain in our hearts forever. Someone may give you the "Prayer at the Death of a Pet" or "The Rainbow Bridge" someday, if you seek grief counseling during the illness or after the death of a beloved pet. If someday you feel the need to visit our

Quiet Room at Friends Helping Friends and circumstances make that impossible, I'd like to share these with you now.

I myself cannot read "The Rainbow Bridge" without getting a lump in my throat.

THE RAINBOW BRIDGE

There is a bridge connecting Heaven and Earth. It is called the

Rainbow Bridge because of its many colors. Just this side of the

Rainbow Bridge there is a land of meadows, hills and

valleys with lush green grass. When a beloved pet dies, the pet

goes to this place. There is always food and

water and warm spring weather. The old and frail animals are

young again. Those who are maimed are made whole again.

They play all day with each other.

There is only one thing missing.

They are not with their special person who loved them on Earth.

So, each day they run and play until the day comes when one

suddenly stops playing and looks up!

The nose twitches! The ears are up! The eyes are staring!

And this one suddenly runs from the group!

You have been seen, and when you and your special friend meet,

you take him or her in your arms and embrace. Your face is

kissed again and again and again; and you look once
   more into
the eyes of your trusting pet.

Then you can cross the Rainbow Bridge together
   never again to be separated.

PRAYER AT THE DEATH OF A PET
Lord God,
to those who have never had a pet,
this prayer will sound strange,
but to You, Lord of All Life and Creator of
   All Creatures,
it will be understandable.
   My heart is heavy
as I face the loss in death of my beloved ———
who was so much a part of my life.

This pet made my life more enjoyable
   and gave me cause to laugh
   and to find joy in her company.
I remember the fidelity and loyalty of this pet
   and will miss her being with me.
From her I learned many lessons, such as the quality
   of naturalness
   and the unembarrassed request for affection.
In caring for her daily needs,
   I was taken up and out of my own self-needs
   and thus learned to service another.

May the death of this creature of Yours
   remind me that death comes to all of us,
   animal and human,
   and that it is the natural passage for all life.

May ——— sleep on
   in an eternal slumber in Your godly care
   as all creation awaits the fullness of liberation.

Amen

>   —*Alan Novak, Friends Helping Friends*

Gimpy Tripod

My cat was found as a kitten meowing in my grandpar-
ents' driveway. He had been in an accident and was
missing one of his front paws.

My mom was a good nurse. The kitten grew and
got healthier. He played, scampered, and climbed trees
and fences. He never seemed to miss his paw.

My dad was humorous and came up with the name
Gimpy Tripod. His favorite things were a wind-up
mouse, chasing mice, catnip, and milk.

He had a lot of friends. His best friend was Schatzi,
his dog. His other friends were Chrissy and Dr. Fitzgerald. When Chrissy came to visit, Gimpy would
sleep with her. His vet was Dr. Fitzgerald. Dr. Fitzgerald took care of him for ten years.

Later, Gimpy got diabetes and had to take shots.

Gimpy lived until he was twelve, an old man, if you

translate to people years. Gimpy had already used up more than his nine lives.

Dr. Fitzgerald said, "God gave Gimpy back many times, but this time he kept him."

I wrote a book about Gimpy called *Gimpy Tripod* with pictures so we can always remember him. It has helped me and my family deal with our sadness.

It's hard to say good-bye to a pet that was loved as much as Gimpy. Although he is in heaven now, he will always be a part of our hearts.

Gimpy Tripod 1982–1994

—Amanda Yoches, age 7, in memory of our Kitty-Boy

Evan and Ollie

My son Evan was sixteen months old when we went to see some friends who lived on a ranch. In their barn were some kittens and a baby raccoon that were orphaned. There was a two-month-old Siamese mix that Evan fell in love with. He brought the kitten to us by holding it around the neck, the kitten just hanging there, not fighting at all, while Evan toddled to us saying, *"Me yuv dis cat."*

We decided that if that kitten would put up with being carried like that, he deserved a chance. We quickly gave Evan lessons on how to hold a cat, and soon the two became inseparable.

Evan and Ollie ate breakfast together and played together. At night I would read Evan books in the rocking chair. Every night when I did this Ollie would come out of nowhere and climb into my lap, or in my arms. Usually Evan was in my left arm and Ollie in my right. As I read the story and turned the pages, Ollie would look at the pages and turn his head when I turned the pages until eventually Evan and Ollie would fall asleep in my arms together. (Or Evan would have one arm holding his stuffed bunny and one arm holding Ollie.)

When Evan was three and a half, Ollie was hit by a car and died. Evan was sad but seemed to handle it well for a little boy. But he has never forgotten Ollie, and Ollie has made a bigger impression on Evan than we thought.

When Evan was in first grade at Montessori School of Denver, he was supposed to write his parents a Valentine poem for Valentine's Day. With the help of Judy Houston, his assistant teacher, Evan instead wrote a poem to Ollie.

It really surprised us that Evan even remembered Ollie so clearly since he died when Evan was so young. But we were happy that Evan had (and has) experienced a love for an animal so strongly. We are very proud of him.

A VALENTINE POEM FOR OLLIE
I miss you Ollie.
I miss you, you see.
I loved the way you read books with me.
You're happy in heaven, I'm sure of that.
Thank you for being my wonderful cat.
—*Evan Vigil, age six and a half*

—*Julie Pfannenstein*

Muffin's Return

*EDITOR'S NOTE: Cats appear in the dreams of
countless people, ancient symbols of psychic energy. But
is their appearance in the netherworld of the dream
more than a symbol? There are many accounts of cats
who return to their owners in dreams as shepherds
during emotional crises, aiding their owners' passage
through life.*

Muffin was the cat who was by my side during the years
I built my life. My dearest cat was with me for twenty
years. She saw me through my lonely med-school days,
and was there for the disastrous end to my first love.
She moved with me from apartment to apartment, tolerated my long hours at the hospital, and always welcomed me home. Muffin had a way of comforting me
when I was upset. She would sit near my face and stare
at me, and purr. I came to cherish her "comfort routine."

I always felt the pets I rescued wished to repay that
kindness, but Muffin showed her gratitude far beyond
any cat I ever experienced. I didn't choose her. Like all
my cats she chose me. I was in medical school, and had
one cat. I heard of a wealthy family in Chester County
who had let their cats breed to intolerable levels. They
invited acquaintances to come and take one; the others
were going to be put down. I didn't really need another
pet, but that story upset me, and off I went. I walked
into a large summer kitchen and sat down on a bench.
A malnourished but beautiful calico came over and
jumped into my lap. Home we went.

Muffin had an infection and parasites. She was dehydrated. My vet wasn't very hopeful about her
chances. I gave her fluids subcutaneously for several

weeks, as well as her other medicines. She survived and thrived.

Muffin accepted my marriage to Ted, and we eventually had thirteen pets. As they all aged together, they developed the usual elderly animal ailments, and, at one point, I was giving out thirty pills a day. We made a commitment never to keep them beyond the days when they could enjoy life, and I think we've kept it. But, it gets harder and harder to lose each pet.

Hardest of all was losing Muffin. But little did I know I would never really lose her—that old saying "You can never lose a cat" is truer than I ever imagined.

In 1992, Muffin, then twenty, had begun to fail. Her kidneys and eyesight were going, and I knew the day was soon coming when we would have to put her to sleep. Still, remarkable friend that she was, she was always there to comfort me.

One night, another cat of ours, a lovely, thin white cat named Mary Alice, was in great distress, and I spent the night sleeping beside her on the floor. She had a heartrate of over three hundred. Mary Alice was a miraculous creature in her own right. As a young cat, she'd been diagnosed by my vet with a form of cardiomyopathy. At the University of Pennsylvania Veterinary School, they confirmed the diagnosis, and told me that with medicine she would live about six months. She lived eight more happy years! A few times a year, she would have one of her "crises" which would last for a few hours. I would give her extra medicine, and lie on the floor with her.

That night her pain was so bad I felt terrible for her. There seemed to be nothing I could do. Lying on the floor with Mary Alice, I broke into sobs. Poor old Muffin, lying on her bed, barely able to move, pulled herself up, walked over and sat very near my face, purring loudly with the last of her strength. Her "comfort routine." I cried even harder knowing how much she must have loved me to do that when so ill.

A few weeks later, Muffin died. In two years, we lost six beloved elderly pets to old age. But, Muffin left the biggest hole in my heart. I missed her terribly, and did not feel peaceful about her loss.

Two years later, Mary Alice began to lose weight. I could tell it wasn't one of her crises that she would get over. Her kidneys were failing, and I knew that another terrible loss was coming, one I was ill prepared to accept. Really, I still had *not* accepted Muffin's death two years earlier.

That's when Muffin came to me in a dream. In the dream, Mary Alice was in a crisis and I was lying on the floor as I usually did. Muffin came over and purred loudly before my face, and told me she had come to help me care for Mary Alice. Even as she did her "comfort routine" in my dream, I knew Muffin was dead and had returned to help me. I was so happy to see her!

When I awoke, I was crying, but I felt peaceful at last about Muffin. Muffin's return had given me the courage I needed to do what Mary Alice desperately needed me to do—gently help her die.

I felt that I had truly had a visit with Muffin, and my husband, Ted, said he envied that. Muffin, great cat that she was, had comforted me even in death. Perhaps someday we'll understand the mystery of our relationship with the animals, and hopefully, see our departed pets again.

—*Dr. Rita Mary Hanly*

The Cat Who Conquered Death

I am the current mother of a dog and a cat adopted from a shelter, two cats who just wandered to my door and into my life, and another dog who followed me home from school. I love them all, but the finest animal that ever graced the planet was Morrison, the cat.

When we met, it was love at first sight! There before me lounged this huge, muscular hunk, his powerful body dwarfing every male around him. He was dressed rather *formally*, in a gray pinstriped suit complemented by white shoes and matching gloves. His enormous green eyes gazed into mine with such intelligent serenity I knew that at last, I had found the guy of my dreams.

We met at the Long Beach Animal Shelter, where Willie and I had gone to adopt a kitten. There the volunteer introduced us to the big, gray tom whose time, she said, was up. Today would be his last—he was scheduled for euthanasia.

Willie held this calm, quiet giant for a few moments (I could only stare) and from that moment, Morrison Matthew took charge of our family.

The nineteen-pounder decided he was satisfied with the "Walks," which was where we were renting a house at the time. He let us know at once that he was a devotee of regular outdoor exercise who would go out when he wished, come in when he wished, and sleep when and where he wished. He soon gained control of the neighborhood—conquering everything and everybody in sight.

He terrorized other cats and bullied any dogs who wandered into his domain. Of course, he took his share of serious rips and gashes, and we became substantial contributors to our vet's new home. He was also a favorite with the doctor and his assistants. Never did he scratch or bite when being treated. He'd put his arms around my neck and bury his head in my shoulder when having his temperature taken or receiving an injection. When being carried to the treatment room for serious administrations, he'd hug the assistant carrying him. They'd invariably remark that his demeanor suggested that he was aware that their intentions were to help him.

Most of the time, however, Morrison was a hale-and-hearty fellow who was quite content to lie on the most comfortable chair, belly-up, soaking in the sun. Of course, it took me a while to figure out why our yard was constantly littered with the corpses of unfortunate birds and why, in his presence, the survivors would shriek at him in maniacal rage!

Our Morrison may have felt contempt for mammals of a lesser order and certainly did not consider fish or birds any more than tasty morsels, but he did adore people. Parents never fretted when their toddlers raced at Morrison as he lay sunning himself. They knew the children's pokes, prods, and playfulness would be tolerated and even enjoyed. His gentleness was legendary.

We soon learned that grilling chicken or shrimp outdoors required guard duty. Once the food was removed from the grill and placed on a platter, a turned head guaranteed the loss of part of our dinner.

While the move to our new home did not thrill Morrison initially, he soon came to love and dominate the canal area. A couple who lived several houses to the south reported that Morrison often climbed into their window to visit. In fact, once when they hosted a party, Morrison (who obviously assumed his invitation had been lost in the mail) entered the house, mingled cordially with the other guests, ate the canapés, and then patiently waited at the door to signal his wish not to overstay his welcome.

He also adored our next-door neighbors, but his adoration did not extend to their cat. One afternoon he leapt in their window and walloped their poor, declawed cat, who he felt was staring at him.

One day a young girl came to our door to ask if we owned the "big, fat, gray cat." When we confessed, she said he often came to visit her family, who lived around the corner. He would jump in the window, chow down on whatever was available, allow himself to be scratched and cuddled, and then take his leave. She and her family had, as everyone else who knew him, succumbed to his charms.

Morrison succumbed, finally, to feline leukemia. Although he fought and won every bout of infection inflicted upon him by the bites of other animals, his body lost the battle with the horrible cancer. He lived for a month with a red blood count of less than 5 percent. He endured visits to the vet every other day. He did not suffer; he was in no pain, but his body became weaker each moment. I took to sleeping on the floor with him when I realized that he could no longer jump off the bed to get to his litter box without crashing to the floor.

At 9:40 P.M. on July 24, 1991, my Morrison cried for me. I was lying next to him, sleeping, and jumped up to put on the light. He had fallen and was lying on his side. His breathing was terribly labored. I held him, kissed him, and talked to him as I petted him gently, telling him not to fight anymore. He seemed to understand; he whispered farewell and in less than fifteen minutes my beloved friend was gone. I wrapped him in an afghan knitted by my mother and dug his grave beneath his favorite tree in our backyard.

This gorgeous, gentle giant who hugged us around the neck with his arms and tucked his sweet face into the crook of our throats had broken my heart and taken a piece with him.

I pray he was met in heaven by Josh and Tawny and Cuddles and Teak and Doc and by all the rest of the good creatures who have so enriched our human lives.

I will not say good-bye, Morrison; for my gentle giant, if anyone could, is right now conquering the hearts of everyone upstairs and giving the Grim Reaper all he can handle. You will be with me here always, my love.

—Michelle Cooper

Opie

You were one of five kittens born at 2:00 A.M. that night, each one a special little gift. You and your brother Gumby decided to spend your lives with me, and your siblings found good homes with close friends. Over the years you remained independent but loving. With your almost pure white coat spotted with large patches of orange and graced by your slightly crossed eyes you burned your image deep into my heart. During your life I met my wife, and now I wonder if it was you who clinched the deal. You so much enjoyed the spring, spending long hours late into the night sitting in "your" chair on the screened-in porch until I had to come and get you in and lock up.

Monday was just another normal night; you ate your supper and headed out for the porch to watch the moon come up but something was oh so wrong, and without as much as a whimper you came into the house and lay down and closed your eyes forever. You didn't die, little guy, you were just returned to the manufacturer. We miss you, Opie-Steuben, and Gumby does too. I know there's a place in heaven for kitties and we hope to see you there. X X O O. Sadly missed by your mom and dad.

     —Anonymous from the Virtual Pet Cemetery

About the Authors

Four times nominated for the Pulitzer Prize, Michael Capuzzo writes a nationally syndicated pet column that appears in *Newsday*, the *Philadelphia Inquirer*, *Rocky Mountain News*, and numerous other newspapers. He is the author of *Wild Things* and *Mutts: America's Dogs*. Teresa Banik Capuzzo writes feature stories for the *Philadelphia Daily News*. She was the chief researcher for an *Inquirer* Pulitzer Prize–winning series and the book *America: What Went Wrong?* The Capuzzos, who live on a farm in southern New Jersey, are co-authors of *Our Best Friends*, the companion volume to *Cat Caught My Heart*.